Fairy Tales for Adults

DAVID R. EWBANK

Order this book online at www.trafford.com
or email orders@trafford.com

Most Trafford titles are also available at major online book retailers.

© Copyright 2013 David R. Ewbank.

All rights reserved. No part of this publication may be reproduced, stored in a retrieval system, or transmitted, in any form or by any means, electronic, mechanical, photocopying, recording, or otherwise, without the written prior permission of the author.

Printed in the United States of America.

ISBN: 978-1-4669-7134-9 (sc)
ISBN: 978-1-4669-7133-2 (e)

Trafford rev. 12/13/2012

 www.trafford.com

North America & international
toll-free: 1 888 232 4444 (USA & Canada)
phone: 250 383 6864 ♦ fax: 812 355 4082

Dr. Ewbank holds degrees from the University of Colorado, Ohio University and the University of Illinois. A retired professor, he taught for thirty-two years in the English Department of Kent State University. He is a contributing editor to the Ohio/Baylor *Complete Works of Robert Browning*. His novel *A Distant Summer* appeared in 2010.

Foreword

David R. Ewbank

The world has long known, enjoyed and profited from those strange and fabulous narratives that we designate with the quaint and misleading nomination *fairy tales*. Throughout the centuries their naïve plots and simple themes have enchanted and enlightened, so penetrating the consciousness of generations of readers that they have become an indispensable cultural treasure internationally recognized and esteemed. No reasonable person would wish to impugn their incontestable value, and yet, wonderful as they are in their unique way, such a person might well, with due respect and without prejudice, be inclined to insist that fairy tales are, after all, for children. We are first exposed to them when we are young, and though we may remember them with nostalgic affection throughout our lives, most of us do outgrow them, developing a taste for greater realism and subtler effects. At any rate, such is my opinion—one which, for fear of being deemed captious or ungrateful, I have hitherto kept largely to myself.

And so it was with the greatest amazement and pleasure that I happened upon the oeuvre of which the anthology I am now introducing is constituted, a body of work to which I have assigned the title *Fairy Tales for Adults*. An account of the circumstances surrounding the serendipitous discovery of these hitherto unknown treasures requires more attention and space than can reasonably be

DAVID R. EWBANK

afforded by a brief introductory note and will, therefore, be deferred until it can be fully and adequately presented at book length in a forthcoming tome which I am currently inditing. However, I believe that it would be unconscionable to withhold from the public the stories, poems and dramas which it has been my signal privilege to discover until the details of their unearthing can be brought fully to light; consequently, I determined to cast them out upon the world—orphans with neither lineage nor pedigree, so to speak—confident of their ability to stand alone on their own merits.

It is a source of wonder and gratification to me that a score, plus one, of major American authors—men and women spanning a range of time from colonial days to the present, professional writers all, and all quite unlike one another in many another respect—a source of astonishment, I say, that such illustrious literary figures should all concur with my opinion of fairy tales (not, to be sure, a low opinion, but admittedly a qualified one) and that, in fact, they have all undertaken to amend the situation by devoting their redoubtable talents to a retelling of these unpretentious stories in such a manner as to render them attractive to the more sophisticated discernment of older readers. Of the many significant contributions to world literature which in the last few decades have arrested the attention of the public, I consider the works included in this volume to be among the most preeminent, rendering as they do the invaluable service of broadening the audience and deepening the appeal of the charmingly naive stories which so diverted and brightened our innocent childhood days.

But enough! I herewith forsake further preamble and humbly tender to its readers this collection of strange and wonderful lore: fairy tales for adults.

Contents

Foreword v
  David R. Ewbank

The Way to Beauty...1
  Benjamin Franklin

The Gold Hair 7
  Edgar Allan Poe

Leaves from an Old Mansion.....................................11
  Nathaniel Hawthorne

The Little Mute Maid..21
  Herman Melville

Rumpelstilskin's Shanty...35
  Harriet Beecher Stowe

When I Read the Fabulous Tales 51
  Walt Whitman

1776...57
  Emily Dickinson

Tale of the Wayward Kin..59
  Henry Wadsworth Longfellow

Princess Viele-Matratzen 63
  Henry James

Mending Shoes 71
    Robert Frost

Jack and the Southern Gothic Beanstalk.................................75
    William Faulkner

Lament of the Frog Prince 85
    Edna St. Vincent Millay

Strange Quartet..89
    Eugene O'Neill

Sweet Day of Wrath 103
    John Steinbeck

Snow White Noir..115
    Raymond Chandler

Beauty and Beastski..125
    Tennessee Williams

The Old Gingerbread Man 137
    Ernest Hemingway

Beauty Abeyant: a Comedy 145
    T. S. Eliot

The Glass Slipper: Confession of a Happy Wedded Prince 169
    Vladimir Nabokov

On the Skids 181
    Jack Kerouac

The Paid Piper 193
    Cormac McCarthy

The Way to Beauty

Benjamin Franklin

Gracious Reader,

That I may make Claim to have become a Name among my fellow Countrymen is not, I believe, the empty Conceit of a Self-serving Braggart, but a Fact which I may assert without Vanity. Through the Dispensation of a benignant Providence and the Efficacy of honest Ambition and earnest Industry, I have risen from poor Circumstances to a Station in Life which has permitted me to perform such Service to my fellow Citizens as to attract their Notice and earn their Commendation. And yet, 'tis more through my Achievements as Statesman and Emissary that I have earned that Measure of Esteem I currently enjoy than through my Efforts as an Author whose special Province has been the Proffering of useful and wholesome Advice upon all matters pertaining to the Improvement of the Conduct of Life. This State of Affairs is deserving of particular Remark considering that my chosen Vocation is that of Printer and Author. In that Capacity I made it my bounden Duty and signal Honour to bring my Readers to the Adoption of painstaking Habits of Prudence and Frugality and, more especially, to warn Youth against the Snares which ever beset its Path. In this Calling I have succeeded tolerably well, yet 'tis little or no Applause I have ever received from my fellow Authors. As a Brother in the Fraternity of

Scribblers I have, it would seem, failed not only to achieve Fame, but even to attain an Audience.

However, I have ever found consoling Compensation for this Neglect among the People, who have taken my improving Instruction to Heart and profited from its Dissemination. On the Street and in Shops, from Apprentice and Tradesman, I hear my pithy Apothegms spoken, yet—so little does Word-of-Mouth attend to Authorship—only the Few are aware that I am the Font from which the Wisdom they quote flows. Thus, such Fame as I may claim as Author is, to speak Paradox, anonymous Fame. So it was with singular Relish that I read the Manuscript which I now recommend to your Attention. It was sent to me by its author, Mr. Cygnet, who, as you will discover, explicitly attributes to my Influence the Success he has achieved. Thro' the Adoption of my Rules for Self-Improvement he has achieved eminent Renown and enjoyed universal Admiration. Tho' the End to which he has applied my System is one to which I dare not aspire, his Accomplishment in his chosen Field of Endeavour is illustrious and indubitable. 'Tis not, I believe, an undue Transgression of Modesty to confess that I received and read with exceeding Pleasure and Gratitude these pages from Mr. Cygnet's *Autobiography*. I recommend them to you now, kind Reader, not only as an admirable Vindication of my Method, but as a Model worthy of your serious Consideration and diligent Imitation.

My Reputation as the preeminent Exemplar of our Age of bodily Grace and Beauty of Person is so securely established in the popular Mind that I need not fatigue the Reader with superfluous Evidence in defense of the Obvious. *The Sun requireth no Gloss*, as my Mentor Ben Franklin has so sapiently observed. Also, *He who beats round the Bush comes tardily to the Point*. And, *A Bee Line is the shortest Distance twixt Hunter and Honey*. In both oral Report and published Story my Rise from Plainness to Pulchritude has been widely broadcast and unanimously celebrated; the Validity of my Claim to Beauty is,

FAIRY TALES FOR ADULTS

therefore, beyond Dispute. *A Fact is its own Defense*, says Ben. Also, *A Climax requireth no Cap*. Not to mention, *Only the Needy need boast*.

In one vital Respect, however, a grievous Erratum has been insinuated into the generally received Report of my Achievement. Whether this *malentendu* be the Result of calculated Malice or guileless Inadvertence I will not comment beyond remarking that, to quote my Teacher, *Petty Pullets covet pretty Plumage*. And, *Spit and Spite have both sharp Tongues*. And, *Many a Slander masquerades as Blunder*. In any Case, it has unfortunately become a popular Notion, as erroneous as it is common, that mere Time was the Agent of my Transformation. Thule is not farther from its Antipode than this Notion is from Accuracy. The Correction of this insidious Falsehood is an urgent Duty which both the Service of Truth and the Preservation of the good Credit of my Name lay upon me. As Ben says: *Seekest thou Help on which thou canst rely? Employ thyself!* Also, *For Tripe—Sow's Belly; for Truth—Horse's Mouth*.

I was born of Parents of excellent Constitution, the youngest of eleven Offspring. My Father was a hard-working Provider, good, just and pious, and my Mother, a Personage of firm Principles which she instilled in her Offspring by dint of constant Exhortation and conscientious Example. Of my seven Brothers, two died in Infancy, and the Remainder (Paddles, Puddles, Squawk, Splash and Beaky) survived to conduct Lives of blameless Rectitude. Like wise, one of my Sisters did not live to her first birth Day; however, Downy and Ducky grew to be fine, hardy Americans. They both married staunch, upstanding Citizens and are now, even as I write, themselves Mothers of large healthy Broods. Among my Siblings I had the regrettable Distinction of being markedly the most unattractive. I was brown, ill-featured and inelegant. Though I met with Nothing but Affection and Tolerance among the Members of my Family, I was early and late snubbed by my Coevals and subjected to Taunts and Abuse pertaining to my unprepossessing Appearance. Shunned and derided, the outcast Object of mocking Insult and cruel Contumely, so bitter was my Distress, so dismal my friendless Isolation that I came near to forming the ruinous Conclusion that I was in Fact a

3

Duckling as ugly as my Detractors claimed me to be. But then, at the very Nadir of my Despair, there came to my Notice the Works of Benjamin Franklin, one of our young Nation's foremost Leaders and most luminous Ornaments. What a providential Day it was! In the astute and judicious Observations of that eminently wise and sensible Man I discovered just the Relief of Injury and Remedy of Wrong that my lamentable Predicament required. Inspired by Ben's steady Resolution and signal Accomplishment, I determined to take him as my Model. Forthwith, I devised and implemented my own System of Self-Improvement, using Ben's famous Method as my Paradigm.

What, I inquired of myself, are the chief Virtues that I wish to emulate and ultimately embody? Upon Deliberation, I concluded that there were but three: Purity, Grace and Beauty. For each Virtue I formulated apt Precepts, as follows:

1. PURITY
   Strive with Might to become white.
   Keep Body clean and Thoughts wholesome.
2. GRACE
   Imitate whatsoe'er in the World is supple, lissome and elegant.
   Practice flowing Motion with tireless Assiduity.
3. BEAUTY
   To become becoming, essay earnestly.
   A fair Face is the shining Temple of a stainless Soul.

Through unflagging Labor and strict Adherence to my fixed Purpose, I at last acquired the Habitude of these Virtues. This Triumph was achieved *in* Time—not, as has been fallaciously reported, *by* Time. I would not willfully deceive a susceptible Reader with the false Hope of an easy Victory. Beauty is a hard-won Goal. As Ben so appositely remarks, *Nothing sweet without Sweat.* And, *Nose on the Grindstone: Notes in the Bank.* Also, *Only the Lazy need look to Luck; the Diligent turn to Labor* And furthermore, *He who hath no Pull must rely on Push.*

FAIRY TALES FOR ADULTS

After Months of Struggle and Travail, I presented myself in the full and glorious Majesty of my new Plumage to my erstwhile Scorners and Critics. From that Day to this, I have been the Object of their Envy and Admiration. Their astonished Approval and fervent Acclaim provide an agreeable Reward and ample Recompense for my unflagging Efforts on the Way to Beauty and serve as a crowning Vindication of Ben's peerless Program for Self-Transmogrification. As that Man of endlessly fecund Wit has observed, *Grit and Grind change homely to comely*. Also, *He who lasts best, laughs*. And, most importantly, *Seek Pleasure in Revenge and ye shall find it*.

6

The Gold Hair

Edgar Allan Poe

I was down in the wasteland of Woozy,
I was down in the desolate Dumps,
In the gloomy and desolate Dumps,
The marsh, it was misty and oozy,
And I was in one of my slumps:
A fortnight of errantly questing
With nary a creature in need,
No damsel her rescue requesting,
No prison pent wight to be freed.

I pressed onward, steadfast and undaunted,
Tho' my spirits were flagging and sore,
I was fundamentally sore,
Tho' the purlieus, vap'rous and haunted,
Were becoming a bit of a bore.
The way that had brought me was dreary,
Ahead it was drearier still;
The scream of the screech owl was eerie
When it shattered the slumb'rous still.

I traversed a thund'rous torrent,
A stream as austere as the Styx,

As the dolorous, dismal Styx,
That rushed by with a roar abhorrent,
Like the blather of lunatics.
Then into the Forrest of Tremble,
On the fringe of the Land of Boo,
Where witches are wont to assemble
To concoct their abominable brew.

I wandered with wretchedness laden,
Lost in a stup'rous daze,
In a queasy, disquieting daze,
When—hark!—the voice of a maiden
Like a lark the empyrean assays.
An ethereal air, pure and dulcet,
Such as only a princess could capture,
Enchanted my ear, and my pulse it
Raced as I swooned, weak with rapture.

Dismounting I tethered my steed,
And beheld in the shadowy light,
In the lowering, darksome light,
A resplendent vision indeed—
A maiden in rare damask dight!
At the top of a tower imprisoned
She leaned out from a lofty casement;
A hideous hag, weird and wizened,
Stood below, as it were, in the basement.

What a sight to bewail and bemoan!
What a strangely incongruous pair,
A beautiful-beastly pair!
"Rapunzel, my sweet," quoth the crone
"Let down your golden hair."
Methought that she uttered a trope,
Commanding the maid to confide,
But no, in a trice, like a rope,

FAIRY TALES FOR ADULTS

Hair literally fell by her side.

What transpired—I staunchly avouch
There was never an enterprise madder,
More callous, more criminal—madder:
Heedless of many an "Ouch,"
The hag used the hair as a ladder!
Could there be a more heinous abuse—
The memory still oppresses—
To put to inglorious use
Those glorious, golden tresses!

Astonished, I stood like one hexed!
Amazed, I was stricken quite dumb,
Astonished, amazed and dumb!
By the vice of the hag I was vexed,
By the plight of the maid overcome!
I was stoutly determined to save her,
So I fashioned a scale of vine
And waited until her enslaver
Abandoned the cruel confine.

Resolutely resolvéd to let no
Foul witch further plague my new love,
My peerless, my precious new love,
I cried out in a fluty falsetto,
"I swear to the heavens above,
If you'll only do just as you're told,
I'll release you from durance vile."
And soon a profusion of gold
Rewarded my innocent guile.

Tho' it seeméd a sad desecration
To employ that gold as a rope,
That fine golden hair as a rope,
I ascended without reservation,

9

DAVID R. EWBANK

For I meant with the maid to elope.
Seeing me, she was sorely affrighted,
But soon I placated her fear,
And anon she was more than delighted
When I whispered, "Let's clear out of here!"

We fled from the Forest of Tremble,
Abandoned the Land of Boo,
And in short, without further preamble,
From the dim Realm of Romance withdrew.
We wed, settled down and now dwell
In a house with a sensible stair,
And Rapunzel, who's happy and well
Has bobbed her golden hair,
Has bobbed her dear golden hair.

Leaves from an Old Mansion

Nathaniel Hawthorne

I n my native city of Boston there stands on a busy corner near the center of the metropolis, situated at a stately remove from the thoroughfare and so embowered by a conclave of ancient custodial oak trees as to be scarcely discernable to the bustling passersby, too preoccupied with matters of more pressing and immediate nature to take notice of so outmoded and retiring a wonder, a large mansion, heavily timbered and liberally gabled in the ponderous and ostentatious style of our grandfathers. Built to accommodate the domestic, civic and ceremonial requirements of the colonial governor, its ownership passed into the hands of prosperous cloth merchants at a time coincident with the tumultuous and disputed passage of the sovereignty of our nation from British to American control. For many halcyon years after the Revolution bewigged gentlemen and their bedizened wives, select representatives of the city's mercantile and professional elite, processed up the marble stairs, passed through the towering pillars and proceeded into the vaunted splendor of the grand hall where all of the myriad contrivances devised by the fertile ingenuity of civilized man to enhance aesthetic delight, gustatory delectation and commodious luxury were provided in unstinted measure. But, as we have been wisely instructed by the prescient

DAVID R. EWBANK

Preacher, to every mortal thing there is an allotted season. Pomp and prosperity, for all their seeming mastery and momentary sway, can claim no exemption from the universal drift of all sublunary creations toward alteration and decline. The fortunes of the erstwhile affluent owners suffered sad reversal, and as though it felt a living sympathy with the diminishing power and prestige of the family, the house fell by degrees into successive states of disrepair, neglect and decay until, in the end, it was abandoned. It stands today, unfrequented and unnoticed, lonely and apart, yet still as proud and erect as a deposed empress stiffly conscious of her past worth, however humbled by present circumstance.

To withhold from the reader nothing needful to his comprehension of the episode I have determined to impart to him, it becomes necessary for the author to so intrude himself into his tale that he might elucidate its provenance and confirm its authenticity. Know, then, that I am the last surviving representative of the sadly reduced family which in happier days gone by inhabited this now abased and unregarded residence. With respect to legal entitlement I am its fully certified and warranted owner, though such is my station in life and such my present prospects that the possibility of my relocating from the modest cottage which I currently inhabit to resume the state and status of my illustrious forbearers is as unlikely as my imminent discovery of the fabled pot of gold said to be discoverable at the rainbow's end. I am an idle fellow, contemplative and studious, a dreamer not shaped by the imperious hand of designing Nature to assume with any credit an active role in the contentious, clamorous worlds of commerce and government. By profession, if by so dignified a name I may nominate the unassuming occupation by which I earn my daily bread through the exercise of my pen, I am an author—a chronicler of inconsequential oddments and piquant curiosities, matters beneath the notice of more serious and learned scholars which, despite their triviality when considered from an historical perspective, nevertheless shed a modest illumination upon the abstruse operations and secret motives of the human heart. My temperament and inclinations being what they are, it is a circumstance singularly auspicious that this old, vacant mansion, however impracticable it be to utilize it as my residence, is yet available for access whenever I choose to claim the right, and this because the edifice contains a large library bountifully stocked with antiquarian lore of precisely the sort to engage my interest as annalist of obscure and out-of-the way episodes from our storied American past. It was among such dusty treasure that I discovered the faded, friable leaves which afforded me my first acquaintance with the melancholy events which constitute the burden of the ensuing account. The document bears no signature and is undated, though the author's obsolete language, to say nothing of the physical condition of the manuscript, is evidence sufficient to insure its age. Considering that the outworn vocabulary and quaint phraseology of the anonymous author might present a forbidding barrier to the contemporary reader, I have made bold to rephrase the original, taking care, however, to do what lay within the compass of my ability to preserve at least some sundry hints of the antique charm and sapid essence of the original.

In the deepening twilight of declining day, upon an eve at no great remove in time from this present moment in which I take up pen to indite my melancholy narrative, an astute and vigilant observer, had there been such a one, could have discerned, wending her slow and solitary way up a snow-laden street in that district of our city wherein majestic manors shelter in snug comfort the families of our most enterprising and thriving citizens, a frail, lonely figure. Its detection would have been rendered difficult not only by the pale, dwindling light, but even more acutely by the heavy fall of snowflakes which descended like a shroud from a lowering, grey heaven. The apparitional figure, once having made itself manifest, would have assumed perceptibly human form and substance, the diminutive form, indeed, of a female child. But there was, in point of stern, unyielding fact, no observer. Had there been a witness to the lamentable occurrence I now recount, its unfortunate outcome had mayhap been mitigated or altogether averted, but no such living man or woman with heart to feel or willing hand to help shared the deserted, windswept street with the forlorn and isolated maiden.

The drab garments which clothed her body were such as might without undue hyperbole be termed rags, so worn they were and frayed, so bestrewn with multifarious patches and so attenuated by yet unmended rents and fissures. Clothing, however colorless and plain, may nonetheless serve its preeminent function of providing warmth, but these ragged tatters besides offending the eye offered to their shivering wearer scant protection against the bitter inclemency of the weather. And as for shoes, it could not be claimed that those of our friendless waif were old, worn or ill-fitting, for the poor child had none. All unshod and exposed to the pitiless elements, her feet were blue with cold.

The child was in the very springtime of her life, but upon her countenance she bore the untimely stigmata of weary care and carking want. The usual aspect of carefree youth, bountiful of cheer and blithe of disposition, had utterly vanished and been succeeded by a troubled, harried look betokening bleak desperation and dull despair. Clutching about her frail shoulders a threadbare shawl, miserably inadequate to its intended purpose, this wretched child of neglect and misfortune made her labored but determined way up the street, striving against the drifting snow and buffeting wind. Clutched in her frozen hands was a box the contents of which explain the urchin's purpose in exposing herself to the harsh malice of winter's icy blast, for within it were matches, the purveyance of which provided their owner with her sole means of livelihood. Indeed, not only she, but her father—a shiftless, drunken brute, wont to beat his daughter whenever he deemed insufficient the proceeds from her daily sales—depended upon the few pennies which her exertions produced for the scanty orts that sustained their miserable existence. But throughout the long toilsome day at the end of which we now discover her, the little match girl had sold none of her wares, and the pitiful wight was loath to return to her home to endure the reproaches, and worse, of her cruel sire. Nor would her domicile have provided shelter to any great degree more satisfactory against the frigid bite of the blustery air since home was a bare, unheated hovel.

FAIRY TALES FOR ADULTS

A minute scrutiny of this pitiable damsel would have revealed a feature remarkable through force of contrast with its background. Affixed to her collar, the only spot of brightness to be found upon her person, was a scarlet ornament, a blossom of the rose tribe, though resemblance to its kind was mere approximation, the material of the embellishment being paper. No genuine bloom could long have survived so inhospitable and intemperate a clime, as indeed could no human. What a poignant display was here: that a mortal so destitute of means should have bethought herself to introduce into an existence otherwise quite barren of beauty, a small spot of cheer and color, however humble and simulated! May the poor discreet flower serve to symbolize some positive moral: a promise, perhaps, of hope—an evocative emblem of a saving mercy that tends in measured, secret ways to redeem, in the end, even the sorest affliction.

I have declared that the maiden was alone on the cold, desolate street, but that affirmation stands in some slight need of modification. Though she alone was out-of-doors, exposed to the ferocity of the relentlessly ruthless elements, there was no dearth of humanity within doors—contented, cheerful souls basking in the genial warmth of the family hearth. These fortunate individuals could the unhappy maiden espy everywhere about her, though all the familial intimacy, gracious fellowship and abundant delight that these glad scenes represented, close in proximity to her as they were, were inaccessible and unattainable. Only the thickness of a thin pane of glass intervened between her and these tantalizing tableaux of peaceful comfort and domestic felicity, but in such comfort and felicity could she take no share. How near she was to refuge and safety—and yet how far! How often, dear reader, is it yet the case that we are forced to confess to our shame the persistent existence of similarly negligible barriers separating the needy from the blessed? Matter, surely, for deep and earnest reflection.

The sad disparity between maid and merchant was made the more acute and affecting by the cruel circumstance that the occasion of my tale was the very eve of that hallowed day upon which we celebrate the nativity of our Savior, He who has instructed us that in the person of the child is to be found the abstract and epitome of virtuous innocence, who has strictly enjoined us to extend succor and compassion to the least among us. In all the rooms into which the passing maid cast longing glances, festal trees, festooned with strings of berries and glistening with assorted ornament, were ablaze with brilliant light, and eager children, blissful in their absorption, were divesting opulent gifts of their splendid wrapping. Lavish banquets were to be viewed, tables heavily laden with generous selections from all that the largess that vigilant husbandry, abundant harvest and culinary art can provide. Imagine, if you can, with what keen, desperate craving the sight of roast goose and succulent turkey, of buttered yam and fresh-baked cornbread, of savory succotash and steaming plum pudding, afflicted the poor starving maiden whose most recent repast had been a discarded crust, shared on the previous day with a pert pigeon in the city park.

Weakened by inanition and benumbed by the wind's mortal chill, our unfortunate outcast lost her footing and fell onto a mass of drifted snow at the base of a marble stair leading to the central portal of the street's most imposing manor. Discovering that this flight of steps offered some barely perceptible shelter against the bitterly frigid blast, she huddled against its hard surface, trusting in the delusive faith that a brief respite would rejuvenate her vital energy. Alas, the case proved to be otherwise: once reduced through mischance to a semi-recumbent position, she realized with alarm that she lacked the strength to rise again to her feet, and yet more disquieting, she was soon suffering even more terribly from the cold, the snow having thoroughly saturated her scant, thin garments. In this lamentable condition of sore extremity and woeful pain the wretched girl, driven by a cruel and implacable fate, was near to abandoning all hope when an unforeseen idea entered her mind like a stealthy, unbidden stranger. She would light a match! From it would she derive the warmth she craved. So bold a concept she had never before contemplated, matches being a commercial commodity intended only for sale to others. With trembling fingers, so frozen she could scarce command them to perform their wonted function, she extracted from the box she clutched a single match and lit it.

FAIRY TALES FOR ADULTS

At a stroke the darksome shadows of deepening night were dispelled by a brilliant illumination: such a luminosity as the startled and incredulous child had never before witnessed—had, indeed, never before conceived. It glowed with a rich, mystic radiance which brought to the mind of the astonished maid, who had been instructed in the rudiments of faith by a caring grandmother, the miraculous glow that suffused the rustic stable wherein lay, in his lowly manger, the Christ child. A radiance so vivid and glorious would never, she had been certain, illumine her existence, the arduous vicissitudes of which begat gloom and grief, not light and joy. And yet there immediately before her was a warm, flickering blaze possessed of qualities so wondrous that they seemed to the delighted spectator to be nothing short of miraculous. The flame brought more than the sensation of mere physical heat to her fingers; it shone with a supernatural excellence which lacked reference and adaptation to the mundane world, a quality of benevolence so munificent and abounding that it reached and warmed her very heart. She could enter, or so it seemed, into the very life of the flame, and there she could perceive wonders: a holiday tree more dazzlingly ornamented, gifts more opulent, and a banquet more lavish than any she had ever beheld or imagined. And all these riches were not separated from her by a thin, impenetrable barrier of glass; they were all abundantly available to her—nay more, they were expressly intended and designedly provided for her exclusive use and pleasure. And yet, strange to tell, so rich and satisfying was the happiness which now imbued her soul that she felt no desire to possess these treasures but was content with the charmed contemplation of them.

Was the vision real or illusion, the phantasmal effect, perhaps, of hunger or fever? I defer conjecture to the reader and content myself with reporting the indisputable fact that the unfortunate child's bliss was pathetically brief. The flame was extinguished, and the dejected, shivering girl was once again cast into darkness, gloom all the more sudden and fearful for having succeeded a light so superb. But she had yet more matches. This hopeful thought sustained her. The delight she had derived from the flame of a single match provided comfort so keen and unparalleled that no prudential consideration as to the inadvisability of depleting her meager stock of merchandise checked her determination to light another. Unhesitatingly she proceeded to implement her resolute purpose.

Again, a blaze of astonishing brilliance shone before her. Directing her rapt gaze thitherward she perceived yet again all the enchantments that had previously so thrilled and captivated her, yet this repeated encounter had an added allure: whereas before the manifold marvels exhibited to her view had been exclusively material objects, unaccompanied by any human presence, now she could discern a tremulous form which, in a manner of speaking, materialized and revealed itself to be the maiden's grandmother. The match girl, motherless since infancy, had been reared by this maternal grandmother who, four years after the death of her daughter, followed her to the grave. All the tenderness and compassion that the poor creature was ever to know had been bestowed upon her by this loving kinswoman who once again miraculously appeared before her dazed granddaughter, but not as she had been in life—impoverished, consumptive and haggard; shabbily clad; bowed down by hard toil and ceaseless trouble—but utterly transformed. Her smiling countenance was radiant with supernal beauty, and she was adorned in the golden raiment of an angel. This marvelous vision, extending her arms toward the girl as if intent upon enclasping her in fond embrace, loomed toward the trembling child . . . and disappeared!

Never before is a lifetime of unrelenting hardship and acute disappointment had she endured pain so intolerably grievous. How stygian was the night which enveloped her; how even bleaker the despondence which descended upon her spirit! To exist for another moment deprived of the warmth and solace of the vanished presence seemed to her a prospect as unthinkable as it was insupportable. She must, in one supreme final effort, hazard everything to recall it. Trembling with anticipation, she ignited all the matches in her possession.

The ensuing conflagration turned night to day, and there before her, enwrapped in an aura of glorious light, was her grandmother, still reaching out, beckoning her long-suffering grandchild to come to her. In that embrace was to be found sweet cessation of pain and relief from all earthly sorrow—this the enamored child felt with a conviction so assured that it surpassed and rendered nugatory rational explanation. The vision was more marvelous, more actual to her than any occurrence that had ever befallen her in the phenomenal world. She could touch her grandmother's hand! She could hear her voice—tender and affectionate!

"Come, my child. Come to the unfailing safety of eternal love."

"Oh yes, dear grandmother, yes!"

A fortifying surge of blissful resolution filled the soul of the little match girl. Exultant and unwavering, she rushed into the waiting arms—into that ultimate and timeless ecstasy that extinguishes all mortal misery and surpasses all merely human joy.

I have implied in my introduction to this account that a knowledge of the existing manuscript upon which it is based will serve to confirm its authenticity. Having now perused the tale and having realized that it concerns itself with an incident which in its very nature precludes any possibility of its having been witnessed by any observer, veracious or otherwise, the skeptical reader may perhaps doubt my confidence in the tale's historical accuracy and be inclined to conclude that the tale is nothing more than the invention of a fanciful raconteur. Be it so if you will. However, I shall conclude my remarks with the disclosure of a singular circumstance. Attached to the manuscript is a newspaper report, printed on paper now yellow with age. The item, unsigned and undated, has been torn from its page, rendering impossible a determination of the paper's identity. There are but three brief sentences: "Christmas morning last, Constable O'Toole discovered the dead body of a young female by the residence of Sylvester R. Mainwearing, mayor of this city. The identity of the deceased girl has not been determined. Beside the corpse were found numerous burned matches."

The Little Mute Maid

Herman Melville

<u>Launching</u>

The strange and mysterious events attendant upon my lord's late betrothal and nuptials provide a theme worthy of epic machinery—matter befitting the storied resources of Fable—incident and episode requiring for their apt accomplishment the wonderful enchantments of Romance. Such grand and noble contrivance being far beyond my work-a-day competence, however, I turn myself to the modest task of penning a plain account, trusting that my effort, inadequate though it be, may subserve a useful end. Though my humble narrative be not a fitting testament to lofty events, I trust I may without arrogance hope that it may prove to be at least a fair record of them, one that may perchance endure to be perused by readers yet unborn. Thus the memory of the marvelous actions I relate may live beyond the demise of their instigators and witnesses.

So, a simple, veridical tale shall I provide thee, Reader. Expect neither beguiling ornament nor felicitous locution; 'tis downright, unpretending gruel I'll serve thee, fare not fit for dainty gourmandizing. But, be ye further forewarned! Whoever comes to my tale anticipating at its conclusion to be in possession of a sure apprehension of the final purport of transpirings so wondrous and enigmatical, such a consummation as might plausibly ensue upon the reading of a fable by Aesop or the hearing of a dominie's hortative exemplum—that man must of a certainty be not a little abashed of his hopeful expectation. There exist, ever shimmering beneath the surface of life's current, be that surface placid or turbulent, elusive gleamings and coaxing intimations. To pursue such alluring latencies, to arrest and force them to a final resolving—such a profound ambition is far beyond my narrow intent! Be it my task to register the deed and hint at its meaning; be it your undertaking, brave Reader, if so ye choose, to sound the depths.

But who am I that I should undertake to record exploits of such pith and pregnancy? What is my ground and warrant? Queries justly put. I answer them with the frank disavowal of any claim to exalted rank or privileged insight. I have for some few seasons served a young prince in the unassuming capacity of constant companion and occasional confidant. Providence has so inscribed the book of my life as to station me at the periphery of great events, not in their teeming midst. You need take no notice me. I observe and notice merely; neither my acts nor my presence affected, either as spur or hindrance to their inevitable catastrophe, the fatal course of events which I now, without further preamble, relate. Call me Innominate.

The Prince

That the Potencies and Powers which preside over the nativity of mortal man confer their blessings with a fine contempt for equitability—here lavishing favor with unstinted largess, there withholding it with niggard exiguity; that this inaugural disposition of assets—this initial capitalization, call it—is the prime and original factor in the fixing of man's allotted portion, determining whether he be rich or poor in native resource; that such partiality can scarce be made to jump with the Spirit of Democracy: these grave considerations are conclusions to which an honest and disinterested reader of Life's curious page must inevitably, if reluctantly, arrive. There be not a few who may with justice chafe against the fickle

FAIRY TALES FOR ADULTS

dispensations of Fortune, but my prince is not of their number, endowed as he is with every advantage to which man might reasonably aspire: royal birth, beauty of limb and feature, wit and sapience far above the common portion—and withal a disposition so blithe, a demeanor so modest and friendly that all who behold him are in the very instant of their first encounter at once enamored of the king's noble heir.

Yet no man born of mortal woman, be he ever so favored, may claim exemption from vicissitude of Chance or caprice of Accident, but must perforce share in the general lot. And so it was that upon the occasion of the eighteenth anniversary of his natal day, Misfortune (a sober goddess who, unlike her whimsical sister, evinces a scrupulous respect for democratic dispensation—impartial evenhandedness which, however, provides man with motive more for lamentation than for praise) dealt our young prince a severe and fateful blow. A festal cruise was conceived and compassed, and the day of celebration began with hopeful omen of fair and bounteous success. The carefree skylarking of merry maids and gamesome lads gladdened a festivity ostensibly favored by approving gods with sun, calm sea, and fair sky. And yet, oh man, bethink thee! The comely shows and enticing allurements of the visible world may cunningly deceive! How oft does the sun rise upon a day freighted with cheering presage, but set upon a scene of grievous loss! So it was with the prince. A sudden, violent storm arose. Panic, confusion and travail ensued. The concerted efforts of the stalwart crew could not prevail against elements so wild and malignant, and the ship went down, and with it many an erstwhile reveler.

The prince was saved. In what manner or by what means his life was spared, who can say? He is able to recall only a desperate attempt to swim toward flotsam before a stygian night obliterates his memory and consigns to the dark Inscrutable the agency of his rescue. He awoke, mazed and wildered, to discover himself supine upon a sandy beach, attended by a maid of surpassing beauty who undertook the supervision of his recuperation and ministered in person to his need with a tender and vigilant solicitude. She disclaimed any part in the rescue of the prince, informing him that as she and her attendants

23

were engaged in their customary stroll along the strand, she had espied him, senseless and inert, and hurried to his side. When the restoration of his vital spirits and accustomed vigor had been fully accomplished, the prince was returned to his native realm, but though he was never to forget the maid who like an seraphic apparition had so seasonably appeared to assist him in his dire extremity, he was never to know her name, and that for the strange but sufficient reason that she never revealed it to him. He knew of her only that she was exceeding fair of visage and resided with a cohort of fair and gracious companions in a gleaming white temple by the sea.

The Maid of the White Temple

Since the expulsion of our primordial ancestors from Paradise, what earthly Being or Condition shall man with justice call Perfect? Indeed, as the Serpent found admission into Eden itself, one may infer with some probability that a fatal fault marred the bloom of human felicity at the very inception of our race. Human bliss is ever brief and evanescent, and so it happened with the prince, as is must inevitably happen with all men, that he departed the halcyon bay of his sheltered youth, traversed troubled waters, met with sore affliction and woeful mischance, and became initiate to pain and sorrow, the unhappy inheritance of all doomed sons of Adam. After narrowly surviving shipwreck at sea, a catastrophe fatal to many of his companions, the blithe and sunny youth whose cheerful disposition gladdened both peers and subjects became—not gloomy, but, as you might say, chastened. Midst convivial converse with intimate friends, and even upon occasions more civic requiring the public discharge of courtly duties, a distrait and pensive mood would of a sudden invest the gay young prince, and he would stand as one abstracted, as though attending to ghostly voices unheard by the corporeal beings in his company. These inexplicable humors fell across the mild and even course of the youth's tranquil days as sudden showers loom, darken the summer sky, discharge their burden, and, with the same abruptness of their coming, vanish.

FAIRY TALES FOR ADULTS

Such a trifling vagary might have passed as a matter of small and fleeing moment were it not that it began to interfere—or so it seemed to the increasingly troubled and perplexed minds of the king and queen—with the prime duty of the prince: the obligation to marry and produce an heir. The royal parents displayed loving and gracious forbearance toward an only son who had never, save in this one particular, failed to please them. With tireless ingenuity they arranged many a ball, fête and rout whereof the purpose was less to divert and jollify than to spark in their oddly resistant offspring a lively interest in one of the many eligible beauties who are customarily present in large numbers at such entertainments. But their efforts availed them nothing. Though the demeanor of the prince toward all members of the fair sex was unfailingly respectful and courteous, and though his attentions were received by the assembled young ladies with an ardency eager and encouraging, yet such interest as was aroused in the potential bridegroom was so general and undifferentiated that none of the hopeful candidates were given reason to harbor envy toward any particular rival. His parents were not heartened. Their son's receptiveness toward the glamour of the opposite sex they were glad to witness, but he who would embark upon a career of marriage and fatherhood must evince more than unselective receptivity; he must be prepared to focalize his fascination upon a single representative of womankind. Such a concentration of interest no court lady was able to affect.

Loath to confront their loving and dutiful son with indelicate questions or blunt demands, they were nonetheless driven at last to the extremity of direct interrogation, whereupon they were at once rewarded with a prompt and forthright response which elucidated the mystery, even as it did little to resolve the predicament. Imprinted upon the receptive soul of the young prince was an indelible image: the face and form of the beautiful maiden who had discovered him, languishing insentient upon the beach, and proffered timely assistance. So deeply had this peerless memory penetrated to the core of his being, so beguilingly and with such persistence did it arise unbidden in his mind's eye at moments both propitious for reverie and not, so seductively did it haunt his waking hours that the

25

youth grew confirmed in his certainty that to no other maid could he plight the fullest measure of his tender affection. But who his beautiful benefactress was neither prince nor counselor knew.

The Kiss

To say of the prince that he was possessed of an insatiate yearning for an ideal and unattainable maiden is to give a fair and approximate accounting of his motive; yet intrepid indeed must that diver be who would venture to plumb the vasty fathoms of man's shifting depths and claim to reach bottom. Some months after that signal birthday that came near to being his last day on earth, I was to discover that there was yet a deeper cause of his strange malaise, a profounder dimension to be fronted and gauged.

The scene: the deck of the royal yacht plying a tranquil bay.

The time: twilight.

"How now!" said I. "Your friends are met below and call for gamesome sport. You are missed. Methinks thou art beset by a grave and dumpish humor. If fellowship or friendly converse may serve to lighten thy afflicted spirit, and if that ministry such as I may without liberty assay, I am thy man."

"For thy proffered aid, much thanks! I am, as you find me, ill-disposed. A fantastical chimera fogs my wits and renders me unfit for jocund gibes and prankish gambols. My mopish fit—I confess it to thee—affrights and shames me. 'Tis such a trouble as has the savor of vapors weak and womanish."

"How comes it thou art thus oppressed? Dwellest thou still upon the maiden of the white temple?"

"Aye that. And yet not that alone. The erstwhile placid current of my thought is stirred by importunate promptings, ghostlier than the homely goads that drive a man to earnest and especial deeds. My bootless mood is such a state as leaves me dull and wistful, bereft of honest aim or firm resolution, and yet, withal, powerless to expel from my mind's eye the memory—if memory it be—that lingers there so livingly."

FAIRY TALES FOR ADULTS

"The memory of the maid, m'lord?"

"Ah, were it that, this eldritch perturbation of my spirit should belike be pacified. Nay, 'tis not recollection of a being in our common world unmans me, but a spectral visitant, a veritable phantom—and that, not of a maid. My memory is of a happening—an event which transpired, incredible though it seem, without means or attestable agency. The incident that lingers in the haunted chambers of my mind is the memory of a kiss. And such a kiss! A kiss that recovered the lost bliss of Paradise!"

"Why then, this odd conceit that vexes thee—'tis no phantastical imagining, m'lord. The mystery is soon enough resolved. The lovely maiden of the white temple—'twas she, be sure of it, who kissed thee!"

"Not so! Were it she, I should have known it. Unless, whilst I was lost to the daylight world, she bestowed such an endearment. But as to that, any inquiry would have been—it need not be said—caddish to the last degree. My memory emanates from a twilight realm—an incorporate domain of shades, it would seem—or, may be, a celestial zone. Whate'er its nature and origin, 'twas such a kiss as seems more real that this very hand I hold here before ye! Realer, yes—and why? Because it can be proved? Fie! 'Tis not a thing can be made amenable to the measure of gross apprehension. It hath the reality of that that's ideal. The seal and warrant of its truth is the high, imperious bliss conferred by its contemplation. Bliss, which, alas, turneth to ash the mundane contentments that distract and mollify the general."

"Thy distress is sore indeed, my Prince, allowing, as it seemeth, neither remedy nor abatement."

"Thy well-intended sympathy is gratefully received. But come! Such a moody brooding makes for little profit. The sun is down. Let us below! We'll join the throng in careless merrymaking!"

The Mute Maid

He who seeks to comprehend the obscure operations of Destiny will unavoidably discover many an obscure particular to induce wonderment and doubt. If it be Purpose at work in such complex enginery, or Chance—how may he tell? So perplexed is the problem, such answers as have been propounded reveal, 'tis likely, more of the seeker than of the machine. I advance no claim to settle a matter so abstruse, but confine myself to an unpretending rehearsal of an inexplicable incident that befell the prince's upon the first anniversary of his own catastrophic misadventure and fortunate deliverance.

The morning dawned, bright and fair, an apt sequel to a peaceful summer night. Strolling upon the beach with his retinue the prince came upon a human form lying motionless upon the sand. All unclothed, with only the golden coils of her abundant hair to preserve her modesty, she proved to be a maid preeminent among her sex for the brilliancy of her beauty. Of diminutive stature, her features were of a delicacy so exquisite as to suggest the inspired artisanship of a skilled and subtle miniaturist. Ascertaining that she still harbored life within her dainty frame, the prince carried her into the palace where her recovery was accomplished with the solemn gravity and strict solicitude befitting a princess.

Once restored to health, the maid was clothed in rich garments of silk and ermine, and, though of unknown pedigree, she was accepted into the court as a lady of rank and privilege. Her comely features and regal bearing were deemed to be sufficient grounds for an indisputable claim to superior birth. Indeed, such evidence was all that ever was provided, or could have been provided, and that for a reason as mysterious as the maid herself. The unfortunate girl was mute! Whether the cause of this impediment was due to a stinting of innate endowment or whether it was induced by the horrific impact of her "accident" (by that imprecise term shall I denominate the recondite calamity that must have preceded her stranding) there was frequent discrete conjecture, leading always to no conclusion.

She was adopted at once as a friend and companion by the prince, and soon became a favorite. So eloquent, so expressive were her deep and luminous eyes, she did not require—so the enamored prince maintained—the instrumentality of audible speech to convey the subtlest of thoughts. The enigma of her abandonment upon the beach endeared her further to the impressionable prince who was wont to find in the fortuitous circumstance of her timely rescue, one

FAIRY TALES FOR ADULTS

so akin to his own, hints and tokens of preternatural design. She daily grew in favor with the prince to a degree that emboldened his parents to hope that her living countenance might at last replace in their son's esteem the image of the maid of the white temple. But in this expectation they were met with frustration. The partiality of the prince for the mute maid, marked though it was, lacked the keen edge of authentic ardor. Indeed, it was one of the prince's freakish fancies, one not infrequently indulged, to disguise the maid in the garb of a page and to follow the success of this dissembling with amused delight. To such pranks the maid submitted with a will perhaps more obedient than cheerful, yet no word the prince pronounced nor action he performed seemed capable of producing in her a reaction other than doting approval. Though the maid did not stir amorous passion in the breast of the prince, a similar indifference did not, if one may fairly judge from lingering looks and wistful smiles, pertain to her.

The Muteness of the Maid

That the maid's fate was perpetual silence is, it must be conceded, a sad apportionment in Life's irregular distribution of lots, but that her muteness served to enhance and sweeten her appeal is a proposition—incredible, perhaps, to common apprehension, but indubitable to those, such as the prince, of subtler sensibility. Indeed, even to the general, silence will in particular guise and upon special occasion be deemed a welcome benediction. The discovery of evidence in support of this reflection will lead a curious inquirer to a source no more difficult of access than Holy Writ which provides instances in plenteous quantity of the oft-repeated apothegm that silence is golden. That silence had been a gift of inestimable value on the lamentable occasion when Eve approached her mate, keen to share with him her delectation of fruit, is a contention requiring no ramified defense. And the seven hundred wives of Solomon, they who by blandishment and guile turned away the king's heart from devotion to the one true God, how sore was the affliction they brought upon the land through their defiance of the divinely ordained injunction that a loyal wife owes to her master the duty of prompt and taciturn obedience. Nor is it only representatives of the weaker sex in the Bible who bear inadvertent testimony to the advantages of silence by their failure to appreciate or pursue them. Bethink thee what trouble the stalwart hero Samson brought down upon his head and how such adversity could have been circumvented had he only refrained from speech when plied for intimate confessions by the devious Delilah. The lore of Greece is also replete with cases equally instructive. To mention but one: can it well be doubted that the long-enduring husband of the voluble Xantippe would scarcely have considered muteness in a mate to be a handicap? Or, turning to the resources of Story for what pertinent corroboration that boundless realm may contain, would Shakespeare's Thane of Glamis have been inconvenienced had his lady been less proficient in the unimpeded use of her tongue?

I need multiply no further such purely negative illustrations, but will revert to my original, affirmative thesis: namely, that silence hath a virtue inherent in itself, not one that becomes apparent solely by pregnant adjacency to its opposite. Nature herself bears copious witness to this Truth. What is that quality of a noble landscape—a range of majestic mountains in their austere and serried array; the long expanse of a golden plain, its grasses gracefully swept by the ever-shifting wind; the rough visage of a rockbound shore ceaselessly battered by the plunging, restless sea—what is the quality, I say—quality quite distinct from attraction of form, beguilement of color, or beauty of illumination—that serves as cap and completion of such wondrous displays? Surely it is not other than Silence. I count not as abatement of my affirmation the myriad rustlings and roarings, susurrations and murmurings with which Nature so oft accompanies her spectacles; these resound with no intelligible sonance and intend no lingual meaning. The silence of Nature awes the viewer, inspires in him a hushed quiescence that matches its abstruse source, for the reason that it posits no principle to provoke dispute and provides answer to no inquiry.

Indeed, it must at last be said, the majesty of silence is imbued to a not inconsiderable degree, as are, perhaps, all things imperious

FAIRY TALES FOR ADULTS

and final, with a tinge of the terrible. What is the end of all human contest and endeavor but death—mute, incontestable death? What the conclusion to all our ardent and inconclusive speculation but death—the final, ineffable arbiter? It may well be for this reason that Everyman seeks the noisy concourse of life's crowded and busy highways, shunning with an aversion near to horror isolate and remote retreats. The just assimilation and comprehension of the speechless but eloquent resonance of silence requires a meditative turn of mind not often to be found among the vulgar. In the prince, however, the superior qualities requisite for the receptive contemplation of Mystery were to be found in generous amplitude and ideal proportion. For him the muteness of the maid was, therefore, no defect, but a crowning perfection adding a dimension of wonder and veneration to the tender esteem in which he held his faithful, diminutive companion.

<u>Evening, Salon</u>

(*Enter the Prince; to him, the Mute Maid*)

Prince:

Ah, well met! I would fain take fair advantage of this chance encounter to have a word with thee touching the marvelous events of this fortnight past, a press of occasions so marked and unforeseen in their nature as to leave me lost in wonder, scarcely fit for the performance of the seemly and courteous attentions owed to my loyal friends and retainers—to thee, in especial. My astoundment must be my poor excuse; thy charitable, forbearance my hope.

Maid:

Prince:

I thank thee for thy kindness. When my longanimous parents decreed that I must at last marry and arranged to that end my betrothal to a stranger from a distant realm and clime, a royal princess renowned for her beauty, I was, as I then confided in thee, at once disconsolate and determined. Dismayed at the cruel necessity of forsaking the hope of finding and claiming as my own the maid whose sovereign image is indelibly imprinted upon my soul. Determined, none the less, to play the obedient son and perform the duty required on me. Thou recallest how, heavy at heart, I sought solace in communion with thee, confessing that though I must wed the maid of my parent's choice, I should sooner take thee as my bride—dearest companion with thy sweet, speaking eyes—than align myself for life to a stranger, howsoe'er high be her rank or acclaimed her beauty.

Maid:

Prince:
  Thy tender glance, as always, assure me of thy steadfast and ready sympathy. But now, behold! Scarcely will ye grant credence to the marvel I now relate. My ordained bride is, all unbeknownst to the unsentimental architects of our union, none other than she whom above all others I should have chosen: the maid of the white temple! Ah, the occult and mystic workings of inscrutable Providence! Rejoice with me, my dearest friend! News of the impending happy day will anon be announced, and civic jubilation will prevail in the land. A cruise upon the royal yacht is even now intended and will follow hard upon the nuptials. Be sure that you, loyal confidant, will be most prominent among the happy train of honored celebrants and jocund merrymakers. What a glorious consummation of my wonderful Fortune that you will be with me to share in my bliss!

Maid:

FAIRY TALES FOR ADULTS

Catastrophe

Now, enduring Reader, I must turn without further delay or prolegomena to a recounting of the mysterious events announced at the outset of my tale. In due course the prince was wedded to his gracious and well-favored bride, and the festal cruise was under weigh. To shelter the newly wedded pair a capacious tent had been pitched upon the deck, a superb erection of orient silk, and to this retreat the prince and his bride retired after a long day of high ceremony and public celebration. I know not the cause of the curious malaise which kept me awake on that fatal night, impelling me to repair to the deck for a restorative draught of clean sea air. Be it what it may, 'tis due to it that I alone was witness to the signal calamity I now detail. 'Twas well past midnight. The moon was full and the night was fair. Lingering by the mainmast, I was of a sudden rendered alert and apprehensive by the sight of a scurrying, furtive form emerging from the royal tent. I could tell at once, so luminous was the moonlight, that this untoward nocturnal intruder was the mute maid! And, to heighten my alarm and astonishment, I saw that she held in her hand an unsheathed knife! Galvanized, I rushed forth to accost and disarm her when, lo!, she forestalled my intervention by casting the knife into the sea. And, ere I could reach her side—indeed, ere she knew aught of my presence, she threw herself into the sea!

I sounded the alarm, and soon all the awakened passengers thronged the deck. My telling of the tragedy that had so abruptly and unaccountably transpired was met with initial incredulity, mounting consternation, and ultimate sorrow. Any attempt at rescue would have been quite unavailing: the mute maid had sunk immediately into the deadly, unfathomed deep, never to reappear.

A sad end indeed to an auspicious, happy day! Ever green was the grief which the prince preserved for the lovely, fey maiden who so mysteriously appeared in his life and so mysteriously departed from it. Though her death cast a long shadow o'er his life, so inveterate was the sun of his cheerful disposition that he was ever wont to stress whatever of good he could discern and to remark that his friendship with the maid, though of short duration, was a heaven-sent blessing. Indeed, even as soon as the morn that broke upon the night of her tragic self-destruction he was able to discern something like solace or compensation in the terrible event.

"Sir, 'tis a fair and balmy breeze that blows this day." He had joined me at the taffrail and spoke with a rueful smile. "It meets my cheek like a heavenly benediction—like, one might fancifully say, a loving, longed-for kiss."

Rumpelstilskin's Shanty

Harriet Beecher Stowe

Prissy

A visitor to the kingdom of Elsewhere during the reign of King Languid the Most would have been astonished to discover in an out-of-the-way corner of that realm, dwelling in an unpretentious cottage with her father, a young maiden so preeminent in beauty and renowned for grace and goodness that her fame reached far beyond the bounds of her rustic and secluded setting. Could our reader conceive of an angel come unto woman's estate, he would have no unapt idea of the exquisiteness of our heroine's appearance. Her form was the perfection of feminine comeliness. There was about her a shimmering, ineffable charm, such as one might encounter in a being whose proper and accustomed home is the enchanted sphere of the imagination. Her face, remarkable for its regularity of feature and delicacy of outline, was yet more astonishing in that the streaming radiance which shone through her bright blue eyes and suffused her visage with an aërial luminosity unfailingly struck its enraptured beholders as a glorious effulgence originating from no lower nor less holy a source than HEAVEN. And yet, lovely and ethereal as was her countenance, were one put to the hard task of choosing one attribute above all others to count as the maid's supreme and crowning glory, that attribute might rather be her remarkable golden hair—magnificent, profuse tresses so soft and fine they seemed to catch the unsubstantial rays of the sun and spin them into fairy filaments of shimmering gossamer. In her presence the very birds of the air chirped a happier, more festive tune, and the hearts of her fellow mortals were lifted and lightened by the mere sight of her gracious face and form.

This extraordinary phenomenon, a shining ideal, was the daughter of a carpenter, an upright and industrious man of moderate means. Though the possession of qualities far less brilliant than those possessed by this simple artisan's offspring has tempted many another of the fair sex onto paths of conceit and vanity, Prissy (for such, you must know, was the name of the charming child who will figure as our heroine) was protected from the sin of pride by a disposition so natural and honest that she was utterly unaware of the devious and self-serving purposes to which her less virtuous sisters have been known to devote themselves. A more wholesome, guileless maiden ne'er trod the earth. Bereft of her mother in infancy, she assumed at an early age, almost as soon as she mastered the skill of upright locomotion, the demanding and diverse duties of household mistress, and she discharged these responsibilities with precocious competence and assurance. She became the sweet consolation of her father's grief, his faithful helpmate and loyal mainstay, and the endless wonder and delight of his life. To the qualities of uninstructed, native kindness and familial devotion she added a keen awareness of high moral and spiritual principles preternatural in one of her tender years. Nor were these tenets mere arid strictures learned by rote from the local pastor and left behind in the church, but living, heartfelt imperatives which guided her daily life and pervaded her intercourse with neighbors and friends. First in the sheltered village in which she dwelt, and anon in the entire province, Prissy became famous for her countless benefactions. Did a needy widow suffer from cruel want? Prissy was sure to appear at her door bearing a basket bursting with needed provisions. Was a poor soul ill or dying? Prissy was there at the bedside, a compassionate nurse and caring ministrant.

FAIRY TALES FOR ADULTS

Was assistance required for some work of civic betterment? Prissy was the first to offer cheerful support and a helping hand. Prissy became a byword for selfless benevolence and Christian charity.

So rare was her beauty, so peerless were her manifold merits—the reader will doubtless experience no skeptical astonishment upon being informed that report of Prissy's existence reached into the very inmost chamber of the king's palace. Receiving the intelligence, King Languid's interest was roused. Indeed, his curiosity waxed so keen that his desire to view the pastoral paragon would brook neither demur nor delay. Prissy was summoned, and in due course she appeared before her sovereign—with consequences gloomy and dire for the unsuspecting innocent.

But we anticipate. Before apprising you of Prissy's further fate, dear reader, you must come to understand and appreciate the history and character of King Languid the Most.

King Languid

He grew up in circumstances the most affluent and auspicious, the petted darling of doting royal parents. The queen, a woman of uncommon elevation and exemplary character, superintended his education with vigilant care, insisting that her son be so well instructed in every accomplishment of character and art of statecraft that when the sad hour of his father's demise came, as come it must, he could with well-trained aptitude and secure self-confidence become king of the realm. Alas, that sad hour arrived with shocking and unforeseen rapidity. King Robust, having caught a chill whilst hunting wild boar in Murky Forrest, took to bed and, within hours, weakened, worsened and died. Thus the prince, a mere stripling of seventeen, was abruptly elevated to the throne and untimely compelled to assume the sober responsibilities of royal station. From infancy, Languid had evinced an extreme delicacy of constitution and a marked sensitiveness of character more commonly to be found in the female than in the masculine sex. Was this so because his mother was the predominant influence in his upbringing—because

37

his father, competent and conscientious though he was as ruler, had little talent for or interest in the rearing of offspring—or simply because his nature was fashioned and fixed by these inscrutable agencies and influences which preside over all human nativity? Who can fathom such mysteries? Though the cause must remain cloudy and conjectural, the result was plain: the young king was possessed of a nature more fitted to the pursuit of ideal, spiritual ends than to the accomplishment of needful, worldly purposes.

The reader must not deduce from these facts that King Languid was remiss in undertaking the obligations imposed upon him by his high position. So well had his mother inculcated in him an exacting sense of duty that no subject could justly assert of his king that he was forgetful of his royal obligations or negligent in the execution of them. His royal tasks were always performed—performed well, if not enthusiastically—performed, indeed, but performed with a distrait dispassion—with, almost, a fastidious distaste. His counselors and aides could not help but observe and remark upon the conspicuous contrast between the son and his father. Where the father discharged his civic and ceremonial functions with an assiduous zeal that betokened sincere concern and interest, the son approached them with, so it seemed, an absent mind and uncommitted heart. Where the father took ardent pleasure in his association with lords, ambassadors, merchants, artisans, and plowmen—indeed, all manner and condition of men from noblemen to rustics, the son was truly at ease only with a choice selection of refined sophisticates and accomplished artistes. Where the father's chief delights were a lusty hunt and an all-night carouse with rollicking, bluff companions, the son preferred the company of savants and scholars, or a contemplative, solitary hour in the library, blissfully absorbed in ponderous tomes of abstruse erudition and arcane lore. The king commanded the admiration and respect, if not the love, of his subjects, and it required no exceptional perspicacity to predict that his reign would not be notable for stirring deeds or daring accomplishments, but rather for steady perseverance and quiet competence.

The earthly existence of the king might well have continued to run its placid, uneventful course had his frail barque not suddenly

FAIRY TALES FOR ADULTS

entered upon a strait and perilous passage. Soon after the attainment of his twenty-first year he found himself in waters so deep and treacherous that they challenged and o'ermastered his untrained navigational skills. In the end, the inexperienced captain suffered the shock and mortification of shipwreck. King Languid, to drop the figure, fell in love. But—O woe for him—his chosen one proved unworthy of his trust and devotion! She was a woman of high station, beautiful and haughty. An earl's daughter, she appeared to be receptive to and gratified by the attentions of a king, and in the fullness of time she professed to reciprocate her eager lover's affection. A man more experienced in the wicked ways of the world and more wary of dissembling and deceit might have suspected duplicity and armed himself against betrayal. King Languid was not that man. Raised among kindly people of good will, parents and friends whose chief desire was always to protect and further his interests, he had never previously encountered cunning and had no skill in detecting its presence. He and Lady Lofty were affianced. The happy news was proudly announced and joyously received throughout the kingdom, and plans for the impending wedding were in an advanced state of readiness when news arrived that the faithless fiancée intended to be the wife of another! Why, one may well inquire, would a woman, born to privilege and supremely conscious of status, reject the offer of a king? Unflattering to her sex though it be, the answer, if one must confess it, is GREED. The spouse she preferred to a handsome royal husband was none other than Mr. Grimly Grasping, a mere commoner, an elderly, heavy-set, hard-featured creature of jaundiced outlook and sour disposition, a man devoid of assets other than the richest estate and largest income in the realm. With him as husband, Lady Lofty would be positioned to surround herself with luxury beyond the reach of even royal affluence, and such was her love of wealth and ostentation, such her contempt for true human love and devotion, that she willingly accepted as the price of her worldly preeminence the life-long companionship of an ugly, mean-spirited tyrant (though, if common gossip is to be trusted, she considered another, and by no means inconsiderable, asset possessed by her husband to be his advanced age.)

39

DAVID R. EWBANK

What might be the effect upon a nature so sensitive of a blow so heavy and calamitous? The king's subjects waited in suspense to discern it—carefully watching their sovereign, anticipating some visible alteration in habit or behavior, some evidence of thwarted desire or keen disappointment. They waited in vain. After proclamation of the shocking news that the intended nuptials were not to be, the king turned again to his wonted tasks and performed them with even greater care and application. Suave and courteous as always, he betrayed not the slightest sign of consternation or chagrin. Was his dégagé demeanor sincere, or was it a false façade concealing authentic melancholy and genuine pain? The people of the land watched and wondered, but no certain conclusions were they able to draw. However, we, faithful readers—we who are permitted to spy upon the inmost promptings of our protagonist's heart, who may examine his mind and intuit even the subtlest velleity of his will—we inhabit a wider sphere of competency and may safely speculate with greater confidence, though a merely human witness must be ever aware that a last and definitive analysis is the sole province of He Who alone can read and know the soul of man because He alone created it and guides it.

Know, then, that far indeed from being unmoved by the perfidy of his betrothed, the king suffered anguish and despair, lacerating emotions which he was careful to express only in the solitude of his private chamber. A proud young man, trusting and truthful, utterly unaccustomed to refusal or rebuff, he had been cruelly rejected and humiliated. His steadfast affection, a rare and worthy gift, offered in innocent trust and honest faith, had been spurned and despised. His heart—steady, loyal, and true—was broken. And Time, which in its course is so often a healer, served not to palliate, but only to exacerbate, the injury. He became an embittered man, and, sadly, the rankling umbrage, harbored in the innermost core of his being, expressed itself in a guarded wariness toward the entire female sex. In his outward manner he remained ever courteous and considerate toward the maids and matrons of his court; inwardly, however, he nursed a resentful antipathy toward them, especially for those outstanding among their peers for pulchritude. This, unfortunately,

FAIRY TALES FOR ADULTS

was his frame of mind when he summoned to the palace the unsuspecting, pure-hearted Prissy who was, were Report and Rumor true, the very archetype and apogee of womanly beauty. What doleful fate awaits the defenseless innocent we tremble to contemplate!

The Evil Elf

It was Prissy's signal misfortune to bear a notable likeness to Lady Lofty. Not that the latter equaled Prissy! So superlative were Prissy's sterling attributes that that degree of similitude could never have been in question; yet in general form and feature, the two might have been sisters. When at first he summoned Prissy to his palace, we may not unreasonably assume that King Languid (who, despite his calamitous misfortune, still retained, anent the fair sex, some residual modicum of natural susceptibility) entertained somewhere in the secret recesses of his mind, a vaguely formulated, scarce conscious intention of appraising a maiden of such fair repute as a candidate for marriage. Ah, but when he saw her—when he was veritably in her presence, confounded by her astonishing beauty, what was the regrettable consequence? O, alas for poor Prissy! The king could see only the duplicitous siren who had betrayed him, and his heart turned hard and cruel. He commanded that the blameless lass be immured in a bleak, secluded chamber in which stood a humble spinning wheel next to a pile of straw. There she was confronted with a brutal and ruthless choice: either spin the straw into gold, and that before dawn's light, or lose her life!

What torment, fear and confusion! What strong and conflicting forces were at war in Prissy's breast! When first she glimpsed him, the king appeared to her charmed, astounded eyes as the ultimate personification of manly beauty. Shyly, stealthily, tender promptings of love stirred within her. Yet when he spoke, when he imposed upon her so pitiless and unjust a sentence, how unfathomably painful was her bewilderment! Alone in the cheerless cubicle into which she had been rudely thrust, the afflicted and abandoned maiden fell to the cold stone floor, covered her face, and sobbed. Great tears

41

streamed down her tender cheeks. Just such tears, kind reader, as you might shed were you delivered to so ghastly a fate. Prissy was a weak, powerless child, and are we not all children, weak and powerless against the injuries and insults of adverse Fortune? Though we may be blithe and contented and Prissy be wretched and forlorn, though we may sojourn in warmth and comfort and she languish in a foul, drab cell, though we may be costumed in opulent cambric and she be clad in ordinary cotton, are not we all, regardless of rank or station, apart from all worldly distinctions, subject to the same vicissitudes of an arduous and uncertain Life—are not we all vulnerable to grief and illness and loss? Let us not, therefore, be averse to the shedding of a frank and fearless tear for our oppressed and outcast sister!

"Stop that yammerin!"

Prissy could scarcely discern through the mist of her tears the diminutive shape from which these brusque and alarming words issued. Her first impulse was to rejoice that there was in her presence another being to share and lighten her lonely seclusion, but upon further inspection of her companion, her delight turned to dread. The misshapen gnome who had so boorishly commanded her silence was the very embodiment of malice and ill-will. The unsightly imp had apparently gained entrance into her locked cell through its only window. Though that egress was furnished with thick iron bars, they offered no obstruction to this uncanny sprite, so tiny he was and nimble.

"O sir! You quite startled me!"

Prissy rose to her feet. Always mindful of her manners, it occurred to her that, though the circumstances were unusual in the extreme and the setting unaccommodating, she must treat the intruder with the deference and decorum due to a guest.

"I am sorry, sir, that I cannot invite you to sit down. My furnishings are, as you see, limited."

Prissy's civil words and mild manner no whit abated the apparent animosity with which the malevolent stranger regarded her.

"None o' yur fancy airs, missy! I'll not have 'em! What'll ya give me to spin that straw to gold, fur ya?"

Quite overcome by surprise, Prissy was robbed of words.

FAIRY TALES FOR ADULTS

"Well, what?" he growled, glaring fiercely at our abashed and astonished heroine. "I aint no mind to stand 'ere waitin all day."

"Sir, I am a friendless wretch. Alas, I possess nothing of worth with which I could reward you."

"None o' yur lies! What's that there round yur neck"

Prissy wore a gold necklace, a modest ornament given her by her fond father, a gift rich in sentimental, though poor in monetary value.

"Oh this! I had quite forgotten my necklace."

"Forgot, did ya! I'm up to yur tricks."

Upon the completion of this rude ebullition, the odious lout swore an oath which not even the requirements of truth and verisimilitude could induce us to record.

"Gimme that necklace, and I'll do the job."

Nothing could exceed Pissy's wonderment that a man, claiming to be in possession of the power to transform straw to gold, should desire for remuneration payment far less valuable than the product he produced. How should a creature so pure and selfless, a mind so noble and ingenuous be expected either to surmise or to understand that the profane, deformed dwarf proposing to rescue her from her woeful plight cared no more for gold than, indeed, did King Languid—that the motive in the one case as in the other was not avarice but malice? Prissy was no more able to comprehend such iniquity than the sun can generate darkness.

Prissy removed the necklace and held it in her extended hand.

"My good man, if so lowly an object delights you, I should be pleased if you would accept it from me as a gift."

"Aaargh! You kain't fool me with yur fancy ways, Miss Hoity-toity. Give it 'ere."

And with that, he snatched the golden bauble and thrust it into his pocket.

"He, he, he!"

Sniggering demonically, as though satisfied that he had just encompassed a feat of surpassing duplicity and craft, the ill-mannered brute seated himself at the wheel and began forthwith to spin the pile of straw into nuggets of purest gold. Prissy's mind reeled! What was the more miraculous: that base matter could so expeditiously be transmuted into precious metal, or that a ruffian so selfish and vile should transmogrify into a rescuer, affording her precisely that timely and marvelous assistance that her exceptional situation required?

Astonished and fatigued, poor Prissy sank to the floor in a swoon and remained unconscious until the first glimmerings of dawn illuminated her cell and discovered to her incredulous eyes a pile of gold beside the now vacant spinning wheel. Delivered from the threat of death, she rejoiced and gave thanks, though the outlandish agent through whose thaumaturgy her release had been effected was no longer present to receive them.

But ah, how brief and delusive is joy in this uncertain sublunary world! Was the heart of the prince softened when he beheld the unexpected results of the night's work? It was not softened. Again our brave, unoffending innocent was set to the task of spinning a yet larger quantity of straw into gold, and again she accomplished it through the intervention of the eerie elf, though on this second occasion the wage he demanded was the ruby ring on her finger, a trinket of even less intrinsic value than her necklace. But yet again the heart of the prince, like that of the Pharaoh of old, was hardened, and Prissy was yet again required either to forfeit her life or to spin yet more gold, this time from a mound of straw so large that it filled the room.

There inevitably comes a time in the beleaguered and sorrow-laden lives of mortal men and women when their hope for a worldly resolution of their predicaments is abandoned for the higher, nobler faith: confidence in the safe and assured reward promised to them by Jesus in HEAVEN—that celestial realm to be discovered only on the far side of the grave, that certain harbor and trustworthy haven where hope is never deluded nor trust betrayed. The attainment of this faith confers exalted bliss and profound peace, but to reach such perfect certitude the tormented soul must first pass through the terrible Vale of Despair. Into that grim defile Prissy now descended. For what release from her misery could she hope—on what succor rely? Even were the self-seeking elf to appear again and proffer his aid, what reward could she give him? She possessed nothing that

FAIRY TALES FOR ADULTS

one so mean and avaricious would deem to be of value, and it was not to be imagined that he would labor without recompense. Prissy bid farewell to any thought or expectation of earthly salvation and resigned herself to death.

The evil sprite did indeed appear, and what price, astonished reader, do you suppose he asked for his service? Though such iniquity surpasses the bounds of credulity, it is my sorrowful duty as a veracious recorder of fact to inform you that he demanded that Prissy, should she ever become a mother, forfeit to him her child! To truly comprehend such monstrous malice, the contemplator must perforce be as malicious as the monster he contemplates, and from such knowledge Prissy was forever protected by an unassailable nobility of spirit, but to the limited extent of her capacity to comprehend evil, she conceived a vague and indistinct intuition of her tormenter's motive: neither greed nor gain, but an absolute relish in inflicting pain upon another living creature. Fraught and desperate, she agreed to the elf's scandalous terms. Why? Not, be assured, because she had the least intention of honoring so atrocious a bargain, but because, given the king's boundless enmity toward her, she had no hope of living to become a mother. The dawn of a new day might bring a brief reprieve, but soon, without resource or recourse, she must resign herself to death. With a prayer on her lips, Prissy forsook all hope of encountering pity or comfort in this wicked, wayward world and turned her thoughts toward the compassionate recompense for all her mortal trials which, sure and certain, awaited her in the next.

The Secret Name

The sun which inaugurates each new day shines alike upon spectacles of weal and woe—upon concord and strife, merriment and misery, hall and hovel, palace and prison. The sun which awakened our busy world on the morning of Prissy's fourth day of confinement shone on no scene more splendid or miraculous than that which transpired in her cold, dismal cell. We refer not to the masses of gold, piled in towering heaps upon the floor. No. A greater,

DAVID R. EWBANK

a yet more marvelous reality was there to be witnessed—not by the
corporeal eye, but by the spirit. That great miracle, the sight which,
of all sights, is the most pleasing and acceptable to our Creator, was a
humble and contrite heart! King Languid, when he entered Prissy's
cell and discovered her, downcast and disconsolate, perceived, at
long last, the abysmal enormity of his deeds and, in one abrupt and
astonishing instant, repented of them. Was it the celestial radiance
which at all times illuminated and etherealized her countenance
that effected this sudden renovation of character? Was it the gold
of her hair, embowering her lovely face like a beatific halo, far more
beautiful and precious than the merely material treasure which lay
about her, glittering in opulent profusion? Or was it the mysterious
and unfathomable intervention a supernatural agency? No mortal
may presume to know. Certain it is, however, that the king ceased
to see in Prissy the image of the base, disloyal woman who had
so treacherously wronged him and beheld instead the truth: there
before him stood an angel incarnate, a maiden whose unparalleled
virtues surpassed even the unique beauty of her face and figure.
Overwhelmed with shame and remorse, Prissy's royal sovereign fell
to his knees, a humble and lowly petitioner stooping in homage to
his superior, and earnestly entreated her forgiveness.

What transports of elation ensued! We shall leave the conception
of such joy to you, faithful and perceptive reader, content that your
fecund imagination is equal to the task. We also feel assured that,
knowledgeable and discerning as you are, you will be in no degree
surprised to learn that the king fell instantly in love with Prissy and,
within the course of a few weeks, married her. Furthermore, were
you to speculate that in the fullness of time their union was blessed
with issue, you would not guess amiss: Prissy did indeed give birth
to a healthy male infant of lusty voice and cherubic feature. But alas,
with the addition of this newcomer to the persona of our tale, the
drift of our narrative, which has just taken so happy and turn and
flowed so blissfully through calm channels and sunny scenes, must
change its course once more. Beware! Dangerous rapids lie ahead!

One morning as Prissy was gathering blossoms in her garden,
what was her alarm and dismay when, appearing with the suddenness

FAIRY TALES FOR ADULTS

of a lightening bolt, the evil elf stepped out from behind a rose bush and arrested her progress!

"Gimme that kid ya owe me!"

Every lineament of the intruder's repellent visage was expressive of depraved and brutal malignancy.

"Surely, sir," the dazed and affrighted queen retorted, "you can not mean to separate a new born babe from its mother! Can there be in the entire range and breadth of iniquity a crime more heinous—more unnatural! I appeal, kind sir, to your better nature. I offer you instead all the wealth that I possess. Take my gold and jewels. Take my kingdom. Take my life! But spare my innocent child!"

With that, the eldritch imp spat scornfully upon the ground and, in a veritable paroxysm of wrath and impatience, fumed and swore miscellaneously.

"I'm here fur what's owed me. Hand the brat over."

"Never!"

Her wicked auditor did not hear this smothered ejaculation, nor was he meant to. But inaudible though her declaration might be, it nonetheless expressed a mother's desperate and implacable resolve. No surer is the universal law that smoke rises than that higher and nobler law, inscribed on every mother's heart, which demands that the safety and well-being her child be the supreme care and duty of her life.

"Is there, then, no appeal or inducement to appease your fury and forestall your dire intent?"

"Ya can guess my name. I'll give ya three days to larn it and three tries to say it. If ya kin, ya kin keep yur mewlin' babe. Aaaaargh, but ya'll never larn it! I'll be back in three days fur my pay. Take care ya have 'im ready!"

Having uttered this bone-chilling announcement, with a shrill and uncouth cry of triumph, the repulsive monster disappeared.

No sooner was the king informed of the fact and purpose of the evil elf's visit than all the resources of the realm were mustered to pursue, locate and arrest the vile fiend. Legions of soldiers and throngs of eager and willing volunteers scoured the kingdom, but

DAVID R. EWBANK

hunt as diligently as they might, none of their vast number succeeded in effecting their purpose until, on the evening of the third night, in a remote and isolated section of Murky Forest, a puff of smoke caught the keen and watchful eye of a vigilant bowman. Stealthily he crept forward and discovered a rustic cottage in the last stages of decay and dilapidation. Outside this rude shelter, engaged in performing a weird, grotesque dance, was the abominable elf himself. As he executed his ungainly gyrations, he recited in a harsh, strident voice this rudimentary, tuneless refrain:

> *Guess my name,*
> *There's none a ya kin.*
> *A secret 't is:*
> *It's Rumplestilskin.*

If there is moral at all to be learned from a spectacle so exceptional and bizarre, perhaps it is that though the malevolence of a despicable, black-hearted villain may be unlimited, his intelligence may not be. At any rate, the clever bowman rode back to the palace to report his discovery, and thus it was that when the evil elf showed up to claim his reward, the queen was armed and prepared.

"Well," he demanded, with a uncouth sneer, "what's my name?"

"Is it Schwarzsnozzle?" the queen asked.

"Nooooo!"

"Is it Smellyhosen?"

"Noooooo!" he shrieked, and, sensing that success was just within his grasp, he emitted a piercing, unearthly cry of triumph.

"Is it Rumplestilskin?"

And expression of utmost astonishment and bitterest frustration transformed the features of the evil gnome, rendering a face already extraordinarily repellent all the more intensely hideous. Apoplectic with rage, he stamped and swore and screamed and fell dead that the queen's feet.

Thanksgiving and rejoicing knew no bounds! The entire kingdom celebrated the safe deliverance of the young prince. The jubilant sound of church bells and of heartfelt hymns of praise resounded

FAIRY TALES FOR ADULTS

from every hill and dale in the land. From that day forth, the royal family led happy, untroubled lives. All of the subjects of the realm were forever mindful of and profoundly grateful for the beneficent influence that their beloved queen exerted upon the king. Though in the performance of his responsibilities he had never been lax or inattentive, he became under the sympathetic sway of his loving wife an altered and a better man with the happy effect that what before had been onerous duties became welcome opportunities to serve the general good, opportunities which he accepted and acted upon with sincere interest and genuine concern. The devoted affection of a sensitive and compassionate woman chastened and humanized him. Before his marriage he was respected; after it, he was loved. The fortunate royal pair ruled in peace and harmony, raised a large family, and lived long. After her death, so beloved was her memory that within a few short years the number of blessed souls honored by the Church for their blameless lives and exemplary deeds was expanded to include yet one more illustrious name: Saint Prissy!

50

When I Read the Fabulous Tales

Walt Whitman

1

When I read in the multi-tomed, many-storied library the ancient,
ageless tales,
When I turned the leaves of weighty books and conned their mystic
purport,
When I communed in spirit with authors nameless and forgotten,
When I grew acquainted with the myriad creatures conceived of
their fecund wits, limned in bold, indelible lines: creatures brave,
craven, sly, silly, puissant, meek, strong, frail, blessed, outcast,
delivered and doomed,
I said to myself, Walt, hold on!
What need have I to peruse these paper eidolons
When I, kosmos, contain them all,
When I know them all already?
These men, these women, these children,
I know them all.
Know them, not as derivative emblems, but as living verities, alive in the
very pulse and impulse of my fecund, wondrous, illimitable being.

DAVID R. EWBANK

I *am* them!
I rose and glided out of the many-storied library
Into the mild Fifth-month air scented with daffodil and honeysuckle,
Into the urge and press, the ruck and riot of teeming crowds hastening
    to their multifarious ends,
And I said to myself, Walt,
Sing!

2

You who build well of sturdy brick, and you who build of sticks and
    straw, know:
I too have built well,
I too have built ill!
You who dwell in humble rural huts and eat meager crusts in safety,
And you who eat caviar seasoned with dread in grand urban
    mansions, hear:
I too have known safety and danger,
I too have known feast and famine!
And you, gingerbread boy, stout runner, lusty, fated brother,
I too have been around the block once or twice.

3

Are you ugly and despised?
The ugliest duckling shall find favor in my eyes.
Braying donkey, yapping cur, yammering cat and crowing cock, do
    you aspire to song?
Sing, then, with me.
Join in nature's universal chant, the ceaseless celebration of omnific,
    procreant creation.
All are enfranchised.
All are equal.
Yours is a primal, authentic anthem to my ears.

FAIRY TALES FOR ADULTS

Are you bestial of mien?
I see your good heart and know your good intentions,
You are no whit more bestial of mien than I.
(Well, perhaps the wee-est whit more, but I am not proud.)

4

Are you beautiful and adored?
Me too.
I admire and adore you, but I do not admire you more than I adore
and extol myself.
You, sensitive sleeper upon many mattresses,
You shall sleep untroubled in my tender care.
You, lovely sleeper, oblivious, insensible,
You shall awaken and know your worth,
You shall come to life, aroused by my galvanic kiss,
You shall rise and discover love.
And you too, maiden white and pure as snow,
My kiss, my proud, passionate, convulsive, unrelenting, adamant,
ineffable, insuperable kiss will revive you.
And you, prince in frog's disguise,
You shall not pine nor fret nor wait for my fond, assured attention,
No spell can be cast,
No curse can be sworn
That can deflect or diminish the puissant power of my peerless,
all-conquering kiss.

5

A little mermaid swims in the sea and gazes, enamored, riveted, rapt,
at the handsome young prince strolling on the strand,
He does not see her, but I see her,
The prince is slender and graceful and godly,

The prince is beautiful, his eyes are brilliant and beautiful, his
countenance is kindly and gracious and beautiful,
The little mermaid is sick with sweet desire,
The little mermaid could die for love of the handsome prince.
What far-flung, fateful effects the sight of a comely lad can
inaugurate!
What momentous eventuations impend!

6

Are there among you those who are slow of wit?
Learned sages may disdain you,
Clever savants may deride you,
But I do not decline to embrace and recognize you.
The meanest thought of an earnest fool is wiser than the cunning
intellections of a mocking seer.
Have you run in panic, fearing an illusory cataclysm?
I do not disdain and deride you.
Henny Penny, Cocky Locky, Ducky Daddles, Goosy Poosy, Turkey
Lurky—
Run to me,
Find haven and refuge in me,
I will welcome and receive you.
Have you sold a cow for beans?
I, poet, have long toiled and schemed and striven for worldly
recompense yet paltrier, poorer.
But I, Walt, and you, Jack—our rewards are grander, greater.
Scoff though frivolous doubters and shallow sciolists may, we shall
be at last the compeers of giants.
We shall outvie our detractors,
We shall outlive our despisers.

FAIRY TALES FOR ADULTS

7

Marvelous and multiform are the creatures of fable!
Not solely in royal demesne and lofty mansion do they reside.
Fable is all-inclusive, democratic,
I am all-inclusive, democratic,
No one, however humble, shall escape my notice.
O dear, fine, gallant match girl, abused and ignored—you shall find
shelter and warmth with me,
O oppress'd, friendless child, forced to spin gold from straw—you
are more valuable to me than whole treasuries of gold,
O despis'd maiden, sooty, sullied, downcast among ashes and
cinders—you are a noble princess in my book.
O lowly cobbler, abandoned by unfaithful, fickle elves—you shall
find in me a devoted helpmate,
O lovely, long-tress'd lass, immured in durance vile—I shall set you
free,
O outcast siblings, famished and forlorn—I shall nourish and sustain
you,
O, O, I shall be prompt and punctual and loyal and true and really
busy!
O, O, O, never shall I cease from celebrating prodigal, prodigious,
profuse, prolific, cosmic, copious, creative, fabulous Me!
Yawp!

56

1776

Emily Dickinson

Country Mice who hazard
City Habitats—
To feast their Full—their Privilege—
An equal Right—the Cat's—

Forsake such dear-bought Bounty—
Urban Luxury—
For Fare of homelier Savor—
Bare Security.

Tale of the Wayward Kin

Henry Wadsworth Longfellow

"Listen, my brothers, to my advice
To my words of wisdom, choice and concise,
Reprobates such as you, in sooth,
Are in urgent need of some homegrown truth,
So listen well. I'll not tell you twice.

Think on our mother, that saintly sow
Too poor to give even a widow's mite.
In our humble cot there was scarce enow
To sustain the life of a single wight,
So she must, perforce—oh fateful day!—
Send her three little piglets on their way.
With many a tear she cautioned you
All wagering, wenches and wine to eschew,
And to be ever thrifty and honest and true.

But you, young whelp, her words ignored,
And what's the result? A fine reward!
In a single morn you erected a shack
Of flimsy straw and went right back

DAVID R. EWBANK

To leading a life you could ill afford:
Wasting your slender and scant resources
On loose wild whores and loosing horses.
You fiddled and fribbled and lived at ease
And spent all your money on fripperies.

When the day arrived, as I warned you it would,
When the wolf came by and wanted in,
You said, 'Not by the hair of my chinny-chin-chin.'
(Your share of the family brains is scanty:
As though your whiskers would do any good!)
The wolf huffed and he puffed and he blew your house in,
And you barely escaped to your brother's shanty.

Now you, you rapscallion, you're just as remiss.
You slapped up a hovel of sticks in one day
And devoted yourself to amusement and play,
As though life on earth were a bower of bliss.
And what did you do when the wolf wanted in?
You also relied on the hair of your chin!
But by merely exhaling he forced you to flee,
And you and your brother came running to me.
To my house made of brick, firm and fast,
Built to withstand any lupine blast,
And here you found peace and security.

And why? Because while you were trifling and frittering
I made it my business to build a safe haven,
Ignoring your jibes that my caution was craven,
Deaf to your juvenile jeering and tittering.
The days of my labor were weary and long,
But when I was done—staunch and strong,
Goodly and grand, my structure stood,
Because I had planned, like a wise pig should,
For future misfortune, for fatal mischance,
Knowing that life is no rosy romance.

FAIRY TALES FOR ADULTS

Now say, if you please, who was right all along?
Who, in the end, is the winner—shirkers
Or provident, prudent, industrious workers,
God-fearing pigs who, laboring alone,
Keep their hooves on the ground and their snouts on the grindstone?

Now you'd better not think you can laze about here,
Playing with skittles and drinking beer!
You'll pitch right in and lend a hand.
You'll sweep and scrub and clean and clear
And earn your keep. Do you understand!
I expect you to strive and excel, see—or
I swear I'll boot both of you out the back door."
But this lesson was lost. The wayward kin,
They of the hair of the chinny-chin-chin,
Lulled by tetrameters soporific,
Wearied by long exhortations pontific,
Open their slumberous eyes could not keep
And had slumped in their chairs and fallen asleep.

62

Princess
Viele-Matratzen

Henry James

"My dear Archie, nothing could be droller that this charming affectation of naïvete, but your assumption of the role of incognizant provincial will never succeed with us, your *amis intime*. We who have long since set ourselves to the diverting study of your ingenuous pose have found you out. Far indeed from being the naïf you so modestly and unavailingly impersonate, we know and rely upon you as an indispensable confidant—a veritable budget of court intrigue and rumour."

Archibald Quidnunc, the Duke of Devonsole, examined the tip of his walking stick and indulged himself with a rather lengthier prolongation of a pregnant moment than would perhaps have been consonant with a more resolute stifling of the flicker of pique which this ambiguous tribute occasioned.

"Delly, *cara mia*, you forget that I've rusticated these six weeks on a hilltop in Cianti. In my humble villa I have only my library, my domestic staff and the contemplation of eternal verities on which to rely for diversion and edification. I was, I do assure you, quite *dépaysé*. I return to you pristine in my ignorance of *nouvelles à la main* and famished for original intelligence. For which I must needs, *pour ainsi dire*, turn the tables and employ you who have doubtless been exercising your renowned talents for nice observation and shrewd surmise in the very thick of the current social crush."

Delphinium Dyspepsia, the Marchioness of Magnesia, perceiving that acceptance of the proffered employment entailed a tacit accession to the accuracy of the duke's sharp characterization, unhesitatingly gave the conversational table yet another determinate turn.

"As though anyone could rival you, *mon cher*, however temporarily *désorienté*, as doyen! I should not dare."

Languidly ensconced upon a chaise, Adalgisa Davenport, the Baroness d'Ennui, the cynosure of her *salon d'élite*, observing this exchange with mounting hilarity, considered how she might best resolve the contretemps with a solicitous but telling intervention.

"But come, Delly. You must not, merely to preserve a factitious modesty, deprive a starved man of the nourishment he craves, or, indeed, deny yourself the frisson of, to employ the crude jargon *à la mode*, 'spreading the news.'"

"Adie, *Schätzchen*, what 'news' you might be referring to I'm sure I can't tell. It is upon you we must rely for *éclaircissement*."

"The prince has found a princess."

This ejaculation issued from Sylvester Davenport, the Baron d'Ennui, a man positioned in a manner, as apt metaphorically as accurate factually, outside the circle of intimates, a man whose lapses and gaucheries had become so habitual as to have lost their original sting and to have become, if not endearing, then, because they no longer surprised, unexceptionable—even, upon an occasion such as the present one, serviceable since they once and again served the function of expeditiously cutting the Gordian knot of implicate conversation.

"Yes, Sylie. We're obliged," the baroness rejoined with a weary smile, "but say, rather, a princess has found the prince."

"If she *is* a princess," the marchioness threw off.

Perceiving that in making this observation she had abandoned the pretense of ignorance, the marchioness precipitously continued, partly to distract notice of her defection in the onward rush of remark and partly to preclude the chance that the baroness might

FAIRY TALES FOR ADULTS

indeed accept the challenge and proceed to expound the "news" to the duke.

"She is not to be found in the *Almanach de Gotha* despite her claim to be the granddaughter of Otto, the Erzherzog Spitznase, youngest brother of Toto the Third, martyred Kaiser of Abfallreich. Otto, we are asked to believe, was the sole and previously unsuspected survivor of the appalling massacre which brought the House of Viele-Matratzen to its lamentable end and precipitated the hostilities so speciously nominated the "War of Liberation," that aberrant convulsion the disastrous consequences of which you are well aware. Loyalist supporters, members of a secret organization dedicated to the restoration of the Divine Right of Kings, discovered the wounded lad, administered timely succour, and were ultimately instrumental in effectuating his removal under an assumed name to America—to a remote urban locale with the barbarous name 'Pittsburgh.' In that alien milieu Otto prospered, marrying advantageously (purely from a pecuniary point of view, of course; that being the only advantage proffered or, indeed, esteemed in his adopted land.) He sired a male child, the father of our putative princess, who became what I believe the Americans refer to as an 'industrial giant.'"

"A graphic chronicle, *nicht wahr*, Archie?" the baroness brought out.

"Too awfully interesting! An 'American princess,' then. A piquant anomaly. And rich, you say?"

"Her escutcheon is quite begrimed by trade," the marchioness interposed. "Assuming that there be a legitimate royal lineage to compromise—an issue quite unresolved to my satisfaction."

"But resolved, convincingly or not, to the satisfaction of the prince—and of his parents, indeed. A royal wedding impends."

"They need the money," the baron said.

His auditors deemed the best response to a remark so tactless as this, one having only the crassest of truths to recommend it, to be momentary silence.

"Astonishing!" the duke resumed. "Can it really be that our dear Sachy is at last to taste the long deferred joys of matrimony?"

"Vows are to be exchanged Sunday next," the baroness revealed.

DAVID R. EWBANK

At the age of thirty-two, Prince Sacheverell, sole offspring of King Oswald the Meek and his queen Ermingard, had so far exceeded that time in life in which it was customary for the eldest scions of royal stock to select a mate and insure an uninterrupted succession that an apprehensive nation had begun to resign itself to the prospect of a bachelor king. The prince had ever displayed an exquisite fastidiousness, a trait manifesting itself as early as infancy when his nanny noticed in him, in his sixth month, an aversion to customary sustenance so marked and determined that she was obliged to substitute pâté for pap. This superb particularity, purified and perfected by advancing years, broadened to express itself in matters beyond the merely gustatory. His aesthetic preferences were cultivated to that degree that he experienced almost nothing which met his increasingly exacting standards. He was appalled by the rude "reality" and lack of finish favored by the modern tribe of painters, and the unrestrained grandiloquence of contemporary music was a torment to him. No painting after Raphael and few compositions since Monteverdi's could he endure. Contact with the masses, unavoidable upon those frequent ceremonial occasions when the royal family had perforce to show itself, produced in him a malaise just short of nausea, a reaction which through habit he learned to conceal, but never to extinguish. After such ordeals his wonted retreat was the salon of the baroness where he confidently sought and found refuge from the strident adulation and bumptious benevolence of his subjects.

Though his fine discrimination and beautiful delicacy of perception and expression were just those traits which endeared him to the few whose sensibilities were sufficiently subtle to apprehend and relish them, it at length became clear, first to his royal parents and ultimately to *tout le monde*, that a nature so ethereal, while doubtless a priceless ornament to delight and inspire, was yet—with regard to those duties and functions which, though lacking in elegance and *raffinement*, were imperatively vital to the continuance of existence—flawed. When it became irrefragably palpable that left to his own devices to select a mate, such crass contrivances were utterly foreign to his tender temperament, the king and queen perceived

FAIRY TALES FOR ADULTS

the necessity of arranging propitious interventions, but despite their tireless endeavour and loving concern, all of their discreet scheming was unavailing.

No dearth of aspirants to the honour of princely approval impeded their efforts. Among the first of such was the youngest daughter of the widowed Countess of Pimlico, fresh of face and well instructed by her demanding mother to be ever pliant, agreeable and submissive; but though she was imminently tractable and ostensibly suitable, she forfeited all of the credit earned by her previously unexceptionable deportment when, at a state dinner, she quenched her thirst with water from her finger bowl. There was, later, the daughter of the Bishop of Blackpool, a maiden of exemplary rectitude in all matters affecting the modest and conventional conduct appropriate to young women of her age and condition, but a scholar so ill-instructed by her clerical father that she uttered scarcely a word without reducing her auditors to a state of bemused consternation with such conversational contributions as her detestation of the Canaanites, cursed descendants of Cain, and her gratitude that the ark of the covenant had proved to be seaworthy. Much later a foreign candidate was advanced, the Principessa Viscosopasta, a beauty so *soigné, dégagé*, and *dintingué* that long-depressed hopes were given a temporary lift before, on the second day of her visit, they were dashed by the realization that the principessa barbarously mispronounced all of the French qualities she so manifestly embodied. Though the prince, considering the country of her origin, might have been disposed to view the principessa's insults to the Gallic tongue with a forgiving eye, the reach of his toleration was achieved and surpassed when, partaking of an intimate *déjeuner*, she referred to the *crudités* he proffered as "crudities," a solecism so fortuitously apt that the very servants could scarce check their risibility. The following morning the principessa was on a steamer directed toward her native land.

These three are merely exponents, and they not the worst, of the eager aspirants who, though not innumerable, had for many seasons abounded in a quantity sufficient to cause the king to lose count and, in the end, patience. Habitually benign and indulgent, the royal patriarch, delight though he did in the beauty of character evinced

67

by the heir apparent, was nevertheless wont to utter, incited to such lachrymose acerbity by years of indulgent but fruitless forbearance, embittered remarks with reference to his son's apparent inability to dispose of a matter so vitally affecting the royal family: the perpetuation or extinction of the ancient House of Schwach-Karten. However, were the endurant king ever tempted to the extremity of remonstrating with his tergiversating offspring, Queen Ermingard, whose doting approbation of her son extended to his every thought and deed, was ceaselessly vigilant to discern the king's impatience and ever effective in restraining it. And so for years the "Succession Question," as the dilemma posed by the prince's prolonged persistence in his single state came to be nominated, remained unanswered until, in a manner utterly unplanned and unforeseen, the issue was resolved by a chance encounter. But for further exposition of this remarkable meeting, reader, you must be returned to the salon of the baroness and to the discourse of the marchioness whose auditor, the duke, eagerly awaits details.

"The bride whom Sashy has chosen with such unexampled promptitude presented herself, an utter stranger, at the king's summer residence, Backgammon—drenched and disheveled, or so my informants assure me. Discommoded in the first instance by a coach accident and, secondarily, by a veritable downpour, she was driven to seek a haven in the nearest residence which, as an inscrutable destiny willed it, belonged to the king. Obeying the aristocratic code requiring that womankind in distress be given unqualified succor—indeed, in view of her wretched plight, obeying the dictates of common humanity, the prince welcomed the suppliant and offered her shelter and sustenance. The creature lost no time ingratiating herself by staking a preposterous claim to noble, indeed royal, blood."

"She's a staring, knock-down beauty," the baron exclaimed.

The indelicacy of this remark and the discomfiture its utterance precipitated in all but its author may be explicated by an appropriate apprehension of a simple but consequential circumstance: the marchioness had a daughter. Honoria Dyspepsia, an innocent maid in her seventeenth year, had been raised and educated by an elite

FAIRY TALES FOR ADULTS

congeries of governesses and tutors. Under the strict and vigilant superintendence of the marchioness these mentors and pedagogues had succeeded in bringing their charge to a pitch of grace and finesse so *recherché* that the requirements of even the ultra-sophisticated were exceeded while taking scrupulous care not to compromise her sublimely perfect ignorance of life. That throughout the years the marchioness had viewed the prince's procrastination with benignant lenience had perhaps less to do with a compassionate nature than with the hope, of which her *amis de cœur* were never explicitly informed but of which they were never unaware, that when her daughter had attained her majority the prince would select Honoria as his bride. In consequence it was not to be expected that the marchioness should accept with equanimity the triumph of a rival which at a blow perfected the ruin of a long-cherished and carefully premeditated campaign. Even less was it to be expected that she should welcome remark concerning the rival's beauty since, if a maiden so polished and superior as Honoria was in any regard the least deficient, it might have been, or so it was sometimes suggested by observers perchance more malicious than just, precisely in the realm of appearance that that regard was to be located. Thus it was that the baron's eruption occasioned a long moment of shocked *consternation*, one magnanimously broken by the marchioness herself.

"Oh, I dare say, she has beauty of a sort."

"Indeed!" the duke subjoined. "However did an 'American princess' contrive to satisfy dear Sashy's exacting criteria?"

"In a manner the most extraordinary," the baroness brought out. "She was submitted to a test."

"A test?" the duke queried his interlocutress.

"When the inclemency of the weather abated to a degree that permitted departure from Backgammon, it was discovered that her ankle had suffered a sprain which caused her increasing discomfort—distress sufficiently severe, indeed, to prevent unassisted mobility. There was nothing for it. A room must be prepared and she must be accommodated for the night. These circumstances, peculiar in the extreme, moved Sashy to conceive of an astonishing expedient for assessing the authenticity of his guest's claim to aristocratic *sensibilité.* Her contention would be genuine, he reasoned, were she able to apprehend the presence, under several mattresses, of a pea."

"A legume!" the duke flared.

"Absurd!" the marchioness opined.

"Jolly!" the baron said.

"And the upshot of this eccentric experiment?" the astounded duke demanded.

"The 'American princess' reported upon the morrow that she had reposed most unsatisfactorily, whereupon the prince instantly proposed that she become *his* princess."

"Who could have anticipated such ludicrous behavior from our beloved prince?" the marchioness lamented.

"Well," said the baron, "the wedding is almost upon us. Before the year is out we may expect to welcome a new prince or princess."

The long-suffering baroness emitted a piteous sigh.

"Pray, Sylie, do not be vulgar!"

Mending Shoes

Robert Frost

He saw her at the table hard at work.

"Why, Mary, bless me if you don't beat all—
Stitching jackets nigh as big's my hand!
It takes no seer to know what you're about:
Your handiwork's intended for those elves.
I thought we'd talked that out. You know I hold
That doing nothing when there's naught amiss
Is safest, sanest policy."

                    "You men folk!
Profit's all you think about. Profit—
That's the root and sum of all your talk
Of policy and prudence. Those poor elves—
Pathetic, shivering creatures—work all night
To help you out. They never seek their own
Advantage. Better-hearted, kinder creatures
Never trod the earth—though, truth to tell,
Such fragile fairy beings hardly seem
To live on earth at all, so light they are,
So far above our world where weighty cares
Keep us firmly planted on the ground."

DAVID R. EWBANK

"Why, yes, it's as you say! 'Tis just their airy
Nature makes them subtle beings, not
Amenable to rules of right and wrong
Fitting for such earthy folk as us.
Any yet you call our elvish helpers 'poor,'
And judge them by our measure, quite as though
Our ways and theirs were one. I'd leave them be.
It's work itself, apparently, they like.
You might offend them with unasked-for gifts.
Never mend a perfect pot, I say."

"And worn-out saws like that don't cut. Land sakes,
I wouldn't give it to the world to say
That Mary Wright knows how to take a gift
But never learned to show her gratitude!
The dear knows how our handy sprites make do;
It hurts my heart to see them in the threadbare
Coats they wear. Those helpful little men are cold!
And they had not a stitch to wear you'd claim
Their chosen elements are frost and ice,
Contend that hardship pleasures them. Need,
Not choice, is what's behind it."

      "There you go!
Was ever such a wife! You climb up on a haughty
High horse quicker than a humming bird
Can flit from flower to flower! You'd make me out
To be an ogre. Why? Because I mean
To harm a living soul? No. It's just
Because I'm loath to meddle in a thing
That we can't understand."

      "I understand
It well enough whenever I see wretched
Want. 'Help thy neighbor.' That's my creed."
"And mine! And yet the best of creeds, applied

FAIRY TALES FOR ADULTS

Unmindful of particularities,
Can be a saw as worn and blunt as that
Of mine you found such fault with."

                        "Mercy me!
You'd argue till the cows come home. Fine words
Won't fix the leaking roof or butter grandma's
Parsnips."

                  "With country wisdom of such pith
As that a man cannot contend. Your mind's
Made up. I see you can't be budged. Be
The consequences on your head!"

                           And so,
She finished up the splendid crimson coats
And laid them out upon the cobbler's bench.

74

Jack and the Southern Gothic Beanstalk

William Faulkner

J ack traveled the road to market, rapt and somnolent, conducting in his dusty wake a tethered, complaisant cow, a brindled, spavined beast with protuberant ribs and desiccated udders, as insentient of its fate as its master was impervious to the imperative of haste. What progress he could be said to have been making was not the incremental motion of purposive, successive steps toward an intended culmination, nor yet the fraught, vacant intersession between a fructiferous present and its as yet unachieved but fated consummation, but rather a suspended, timeless hiatus in which futurity appears already to have been, by the mere potency of each moment's stolid persistence, accomplished. Such of his neighbors as those who commiserated with the hapless matriarch whose sole offspring and predestinate infliction he was (and their number was preponderant) regarded him as a dreamer, an appellation intending, not flattery, not mitigation of sentence, but settled disdain for what in their opinion (parochial, strict, rough-cast by hard experience) they held to be his inborn, immitigable shiftlessness. He met contempt with an equable indifference, less because he was impervious to condescension or condemnation than because his indifference to them was so utter that he did not—could not—notice them. The very dreamy, distrait disengagement which provoked scorn protected him like a shield, not only from acknowledging, but even from becoming cognizant of its existence.

His destination was Booneyville, the seat, judicial and commercial, of Yahoopedicular County, land first possessed and settled in dateless eld by autochthonous Chickpeas (though less settled than transiently enjoyed by the peripatetic hunting people that the tribe then was, and not so much possessed as simply accepted by them, propertyless and unaquisitive); then settled in earnest by sedentary farming folk (who, though neither ambitious of pretentious advancement nor covetous of conspicuous pelf were nonetheless tenacious in their obduracy to have and to hold, and who did not scruple first to conceive of and then to employ against an inebriate Chief Ipecac the stratagem of hoodwinking him into signing away his land (even though the land was his to sign away only by right of aboriginal, God-given usufruct, and even though he was as innocent of letters as a newborn and could signal his besotted approval only by scratching a cross—and even that accomplished only because his unsteady hand was guided by old Pappy Sowpen, major architect of the stratagem and first mayor of Booneyville); and yet later amassed, expropriated and overseen by a regnant aristocracy, jealous of status and prideful of genteel distinctions and accomplishments—trills and appoggiatura to a ground base of involuntary, extorted labor—a self-esteeming plutocracy which asseverated and defended its worth, its very existence, with a pugnacious valor that in the sequent upshot did not prevail against its foes in the internecine struggle which constricted and convulsed the nation, a struggle which, if it did not end in a veridical union, ended at least on law books the shame and dishonor of bondage; and ultimately overtaken and overrun by the Dopes, a race of baseborn, myriad men and their endurant womenfolk, fecund and slatternly—a resistant, indomitable stock which in time inhabited hardscrabble leaseholds and paintless hovels in flats and recesses the reach of the entire county—potent progenitors, their get recapitulative and immutable, successive avatars of an adamantine archetype.

FAIRY TALES FOR ADULTS

Jack was a Dope. It was only the most exigent and execrable of plights that drove his longanimous dam to the extremity of sending so unseasoned an innocent to market, so sappy and insapient a stripling, utterly unmindful of the immemorial arts of dickering, dodging, evasion and deception of which the indigenes of the county were confident and practiced exponents—admired accomplishments the acquisition of which was ever their chief ambition and the mastery of which, the indispensable component of their self-esteem. It was just such a seasoned and sagacious horse trader who sighted Jack as he neared Booneyville's town square. In was (albeit neither of them was ever to suspect the connection) another Dope, Hawken ("Hawk") Dope, Jack's remote kinsman, though so extended, involute, and interpenetrating were the multifarious alliances and mergings of the clan, so inapprehensible and inextricable the bonds of consanguinity that no exact degree of kinship could be determined, nor was such determination ever attempted, even by such Dopes as intermarried—nor, given the impossibility of demonstrating either their illegality or immorality, were such alliances ever interdicted. Thus the rife and prolific Dopes grew ever Dopier.

Hawk Dope, exceptional among his kind, was a shrewd, mendacious, ruthless, resolved, pertinacious sharper and self-promoter, an inveterate inveigler who, together with a handful of immediate kin, infiltrated and ultimately inhabited (infested, his legion enemies contended) every prominent position—mercantile, political and even social—in the county and by dint of subterfuge and downright delict became, not respected, but established—immovably ensconced in the security of his genuine wealth and spurious superiority, and in the settled disrepute and covert envy of his neighbors.

All occasions being propitious for the vaunt and exercise of the immitigable cupidity and cunning that was in his nature reflex and habitual, Hawk was no more able to pass the preeminently gull-able Jack unconfronted and unmulcted than a rapacious wolf can display temperance in a sheepcote.

"Howdy, yung'un. I be dog if that'ere bossie yur leadin haint a fine un."

"This'ere's not Bossie. She's Blossom."

77

"Why sho. I never knowed her proper name. You studyin' to get shut of 'er at Sat-day market?"

"Ma needs cash mor'an milk. Pantry's bare."

Hawk hunkered on his haunches, a requisite preliminary to any huddle or haggle, a rural rite anciently established and unfailingly observed by every Yahoopedicularian. Jack, not so much the natural that he could not comprehend and conform to the venerable usages of his locale, reciprocated by assuming a crouching position.

"I kin spare ya the bother uv haulin' 'er ta Booneyville. Durn'd ef I haint taken a shine to that'ere cow."

"Kaint giver ta ya. Gotta sell 'er."

"Why, buyin's what I'm aimin' at, boy. How much?"

"Four dollar."

With the declaration of this extortionate sum Jack displayed the full panoply of his negotiatory arts and expended his entire resource of guile.

"Sold."

Hawk spat. The projectile—tawny-tinted by the residue of tobacco juice which ever lingered in his mouth even in those exceptional intervals like the present one during which a quid itself was not being sedulously pulped, savored and expelled—landed in the dust between them where it globed, shrank and was at last absorbed into the acquiescent, indifferent earth. This act too, more than a mere instance of corporeal need, performed a hoary, commonplace service in the ingrained rituals of bargaining and postulated the meaning that the relentless obduracy of his opponent had driven the disgusted expectorator to the hated extremity of accepting a deal advantageous to his, the opponent's, interests and ruinous to his, the expectorator's, own. No man versed in the conventions of swindle and chicane would have been so naïve as to believe that this obligatory display of chagrin was more than a vacant charade, but Jack was not such a man. Though time-honored tradition demanded an impassively stoic response to either defeat or triumph in such commercial transactions as had transpired between the two, and though Jack was not so ingenuous as to be insensible to the demand, such was his astonishment that he was grinning and cachinnating in a manner which did not entirely stop short of gloating before a tardy remembrance of the composure expected on such an occasion checked his vivacity and he reassumed the staid demeanor stipulated by entrenched and confirmed custom.

"Where's yur money?"

"Right chere."

In Hawk's horny, weathered hand lay five beans, produced from his shirt pocket and proffered with an assured insouciance that seemed to anticipate and accept no demur.

"Get outen here! Beans haint money."

"And these haint no beans. These shere's *mag*ic beans. Bought 'em offen a drummer fur eight dollar. Durned ef they haint better'n cash. Reckon yur getting the better a me this mornin'. You'll never regret it a-tall."

Hawk deposited the paltry, scant legumes in Jack's open palm, seized the rope to which the impassive cow was tethered, and departed with that degree of dispatch that a bovine pace permits, leaving Jack, irresolute and indecisive, assailed by mingled bafflement, wonder and apprehension. Whether adulation for his accomplishment or scorn for his hebetude would await him upon his return was a conundrum which clouded his brain like an insistent, impenetrable mist as he made his abstracted, hasteless way toward home.

He was gone again. So multifold and incessant had the bewildering astonishments assailing her in the brief interval of a few swift days become that she had been rendered incapable of summoning (or indeed, as it sometimes seemed to her, even of remembering) reactions more appropriate to the emergent occasions than a stupefied incredulity—a skeptical, benumbed abeyance of all the wonted responses on which she had reflexively relied before the shock of surprise struck at the root of her impulsive faculty and froze it as suddenly and surely as winter freezes the potency of vegetative life. Surprise merely, not despair. Because, after the first, the successive shocks had been the reverse of unfortunate. Indeed, by the enforced exercise of stoical endurance she had become so schooled in acceding to adversity, so habituated to confronting the onslaught and vicissitude of intractable circumstance with indomitable, obstinate sufferance, that further tribulation would have been, if not more welcome, then less disquieting because less unusual. Notable though not preeminent (Jack was later to lay indisputable claim to that distinction) among her cares had been her man, Jeremiah ("Jug") Dope, sawn in two when, drunk, impelled by a congenital temerity which did not require the exacerbation of inebriation but which was seldom displayed without it, he fought over a debt on one dollar and fifty cents owed to a fellow mill worker, an obligation incurred when Jug's boar hound lost a fight to the coworker's bull terrier but contested by Jug on the grounds that previous to the engagement his hound had been furtively and perfidiously poisoned so that it displayed unwonted languor and lack of aggression throughout the fray and died (whether of wounds or of arsenic was an issue in dispute) abruptly after the contest—fought pertinaciously, mulishly, against all odds, apparently with no hope of prevailing, knowing that his opponent outweighed him by more than a hundred pounds and was by reputation and in proven fact a skilled pugilist—asserted and defended his cause with a furious, purblind insistence as though the outlay, against conviction and conscience, of one dollar and fifty cents were a matter of gravest moment, the violation of a sacrosanct principle so beyond the expedients of compromise or negotiation that its defense demanded the risk of his life and, in fatal earnest, entailed the loss of his life when, stooping to grasp a crowbar with which to brain his adversary, Jug missed his footing and fell into the inexorable, implacable teeth of the buzzing saw. Her grief, adulterated as it was by indignation that her mate had been so witlessly belligerent, was nonetheless sincere, but never so consuming as to occlude the realization that the untimely, inauspicious demise of her spouse in the seventh month of their marriage conferred a collateral blessing: she was spared from that ancient, eternal curse which afflicted and prematurely killed hecatombs of her fellow countrywomen—annual childbirth. To be sure, she had had to confront alone, with neither support not succor from a helpmate, all the hardship and mischance

FAIRY TALES FOR ADULTS

that constitute the common lot of those who till and tend the recalcitrant, exacting, pitiless land (blight, drought, and pests (aphids, weevils, revenuers)), and even after her sole offspring reached the age at which it was not unreasonable to expect that he might at last lighten her burdens and put to some profitable use the meager wit with which he had been endowed, and, even later, when it became incontrovertibly manifest that such expectations (no matter how earnest the exhortation to greater effort, how excoriating the reprimand for insufferable indolence, or how frequent and condign the chastisement for repeated dereliction) were never to fructify, even then she resolutely counted the fact that there was but a single male being in her life, not as a blessing, but as such a welcome mitigation of possible misery as would render railing against adverse fortune or malign providence an act of ignoble ingratitude. Then, in the declining years of her arduous, irreproachable life calamity befell (the crops failed, the roof fell in, the pigs took sick and died, the neighbor's dog ate the chickens, her rheumatism flared up, taxes doubled, and Jack grew daily taller, hungrier, and less industrious), a time of inordinate trouble, a veritable apotheosis of affliction, an evil season of Hydra-headed misfortune so severe and unremitting that, driven to a desperate contrivance by merciless need (indeed, by imminent starvation) and too weak to make the journey herself (insuperably, indefatigably maternal, she habitually allotted to her impercipient, impassive son the larger share of the few miserable orts she was able to provide for their sustenance) she entrusted Jack, who had just reached young manhood, with the charge of selling the milk cow for cash, and Jack betrayed the trust.

That from its illimitable resource of abounding and heterogeneous surprise, distress, and misfortune an implacable destiny should have prepared this fatal unfoldment of its inscrutable design, this preeminent insult to her resolute and unwavering spirit: that a valuable beast be bartered for beans—such a blow could be neither overcome nor outlasted. "Fool!" With a powerful swipe she smote her errant offspring who tumbled headlong into a ditch where the inutile beans fell from his hand and lay scattered on the indifferent, all-embracing earth. With this single eruption of rage and renunciation—definitive, supreme, final—she expressed and expended that last dram of her anger. She turned from her prostrate son to face (with a submissive sensation not unlike peace, not indeed utterly distinguishable from gratitude) death, perceiving that though misfortune be inexhaustible, mortal man's sufferance of its inflictions—however strenuously contested by his struggle to endure, his will to prevail—is nonetheless limited by the brevity of his ephemeral lifespan.

But it was not death that was to be her immediate lot, but an utterly unanticipated and virtually inapprehensible chapter of stark, stupefying wonder. For two successive days Jack disappeared and, in the evening, reappeared spinning a yarn of a celestial manor which he had reached by ascending a gargantuan beanstalk, a dwelling in the clouds inhabited by a wealthy, witless giant whom Jack—dim, idle, unenterprising, gullible, guileless, inept Jack—outmaneuvered and robbed. This narrative occasioned dumbstruck awe and would have provoked disbelief and reprimand were it not for the fact that all skepticism was irrefutably controverted by the palpable presence of an immense stalk just outside the kitchen window, of a burlap sack crammed with coin, and of a thaumaturgic hen which assiduously produced golden eggs on demand. At a stroke the long-enduring, sore-afflicted widow became the incredulous beneficiary of a transmogrifying deliverance—a manumission from dire penury and imminent starvation—an elevation to an estate of such unexampled and improbable prosperity that, though it could be recognized, it could not in truth (at least not immediately, and conceivably not even eventually) be realized—and this through the unprecedented efforts of her shiftless son who (in defiance of her counsel that the surfeit of wealth they now possessed required no augmentation, and despite her fretful insistence upon the danger to which he would by any further expedition be needlessly exposed) was gone again.

It smells different. Like the times before. A funny smell. Not chicken. Not pig. Different.

FAIRY TALES FOR ADULTS

"Set down," she says. "Eat them two cows ya killed. They've been aturnin' on the spit hours now. Set! Hush all yur fee'in and fie'in fo I smacks ya. Yur smellin' yur supper!"

I eat. Meat's pink and runny. Bones, hard and crunchy. Belly's full. My eyes get to feelin' slow and heavy-like.

"Wife, more moonshine. And fetch my harp"

"You and that everlasting harp. Kaint hear enough of it, kin ya? There! Mind ya don't get so boozed-up ya nod off and keel over on it. Aint yur thick skull I mind, but ya might could smash the harp. That's worth sumthin'. It's gold."

There was gold in the sacks. Two sacks. Big, brown ones. Gunnysacks. Where'd they get to?

A funny smell then too. Chicken, she said. Forty chickens. <u>Forty</u> means <u>lots</u>. I can count. <u>One</u>. And <u>two</u>. And <u>three</u>. Then <u>lots</u>.

Chicken meat's white and brown. Bones are tiny. Pick yur teeth with 'em.

I looked in the oven for the smell. Chickens.

There was the smell that wasn't chickens. Then, no sacks.

A funny running sound though. Fast. Closer, then far away.

Harp sounds pretty.

"Play."

It plays some more. Pretty. It's music. It plays and plays when I say "play."

I lay my head on the table. My head is heavy now. There are bones on the table. Chicken bones.

I didn't eat my brown hen. She wasn't to eat. She laid. Eggs. Gold eggs.

Where did she go?

That smell again

"That's pig yur sniffin'," she said. "It's them ten pigs ya slaughtered. Supper's cumin'."

I looked in the oven. Pigs. Lots.

I looked in barrels for the smell that wasn't pigs. And under the table. And up the chimney. Nothing.

Then the brown hen wasn't there.

Everywhere—empty.

The pictures in my head are swimming. They are running out. Going, going. My head is getting empty.

"Master! Master! Save me!"

The harp isn't playing. It is under the arm of the smell. Not a chicken. Not a pig. Not a cow. A boy. Running.

I run to catch him. I can eat boy.

The floor comes up and hits my head.

Pictures are in my head again. Lots of pictures. Swimming, dizzy pictures.

The boy is far away now. I see him at the end of the road. Running.

I run.

He is climbing down a fat green rope, with leaves.

"Master!"

The sound is far away.

I climb down too.

Another sound. A funny sound.

Chop. Chop. Chop.

Lament of the Frog Prince

Edna St. Vincent Millay

The folk who populate the tales
From which we moral lessons draw
Are simple sorts who illustrate
Some trite cliché, some worn-out saw.

Pruned must be life's wild excess
That, purged of rich reality,
It be fit fare for trusting tots.
A case in point? Consider me.

The standard story goes like this:
A royal prince, the nation's pride,
Meets with a wicked witch and is
Into a frog transmogrified.

But should a damsel deign to kiss
So loathly an amphibian,
That signal act would break the spell.
Voila! The frog's a prince again.

DAVID R. EWBANK

He meets a princess, weeping, woeful,
Grieved by the merest bagatelle:
While playing with a golden ball,
Into a brimming fount it fell.

He volunteers to fetch the toy
But only on the strict condition
That she must kiss his warty lips
Should he complete his watery mission.

He does the deed, but she adopts
A huffy, haughty attitude:
Ne'er will she kiss so vile a wight.
What glaring, gross ingratitude!

To get that kiss 'twas task as hard
As thread a camel through a needle.
The prince must ply, persuade, insist,
Implore, entreat, cajole and wheedle.

At length, but not because 'twas right,
And not because he was less abhorred,
But in an absent-minded mood
She bestowed on the frog his just reward.

And there before her stood a prince.
"What bliss," she cried, "what rapture this is!"
Before—begrudged a single buss,
After—covered with her kisses!

Such is the form the story's taken,
But take it from me, the prince, it's skewed.
A fuller, fairer narrative
Would my side of the tale include.

FAIRY TALES FOR ADULTS

That I my rescuer must marry,
Were one to free me from the jinx,
Was stipulation of the curse,
So I had to wed the thankless minx.

But since the kiss I'd earned was cool,
Perfunctory, reluctant—late,
My erstwhile fondness for the maid
Had turned to bitter scorn and hate.

And so you see: the fate of folk
In fairy tales, or bliss or rue,
Is not a simple issue, but
Depends upon your point of view.

88

Strange Quartet

Eugene O'Neill

*S*cene: *The front room of a robber's den located in a wooded area a mile or so from Bremen, New Jersey. In the middle of the rear wall is an improvised bar—a buffet so placed that one assuming the role of bartender might walk behind it to serve drinks. Atop the buffet are numerous bottles and glasses. Behind this bar a dingy beige curtain hangs over an entryway connecting the front room to a hallway beyond. This entry and a door on the right wall leading outside are the only visible entrances to the room. Two shabby easy chairs are placed before a fireplace located on the left wall. The mantle of this fireplace, like the buffet, is cluttered with bottles and glasses. A heavy wooden table dominates center stage. Around this table, placed at irregular intervals, are five chairs, no two alike.*

A large window to the right of the outside door lets in the bright afternoon light of a fine summer day, though this illumination is considerably attenuated by the layer of grime that has been permitted to accumulate upon the glass. Beneath the window is a big wooden chest. Everywhere there are signs of neglect and decay. Upon closer inspection, however, a perceptive observer might also notice certain indications of a game if unavailing effort to "dress up" the place. Various feminine touches (muslin curtains, tatty and unlaundered; a frayed lace tablecloth; a vase of flowers which, despite the fact that they are made of paper, look thirsty and faded; cross-stitched, grease-stained antimacassars on the two easy chairs; a cheap print of Constable's "Haywain" hanging at a rakish angle of the back wall) are discernable, but these modest efforts at homemaking and beautification would seem to have been long since abandoned.

TABATHA ("TABBY") MOUSER enters stage rear, pours herself a drink and walks to the window. A tall Negress with gray hair, she is in her sixties. She moves with a certain lissome self-assurance as though, despite age and arthritis, she is aware of having retained a remnant of sexual allure. She wears a print dress (scarlet poppies against a black background) and enough jewelry for two or three women (several bracelets on both wrists, large hoop earrings, three gold necklaces of different lengths, and a "diamond" encrusted brooch in the shape of a valentine pinned to her breast)

TABBY: Wheah dat man be! He lef' early dis mornin' fer town an' been gone now six, seben hour. An' Ole Jen feelin' so po'ly an' needin' dat med'cin. Dat Cocky's de dwadlin'est, hurry-up-hatin'est slowpoke Ah *evah* see. (*She walks to the table, sits on a chair and, taking a long swallow from her glass, expels a contented, heart-felt Aaaaah!*)

BEN ("ROVER") BERNARD enters through the outside door. Born and raised in the Bronx, he is the grizzled, bearded veteran of many an ocean voyage—a hulking, massively muscled old sea dog. He wears heavy boots, canvas trousers in need of washing, and a coarse cotton shirt so unbuttoned as to display his hairy chest.

TABBY: Who dat? (*Turning, she sees Rover.*) Oh, i'chew. Ah'z spectin' Cocky.

ROVER: Dat ole soak. Off on one uv 'is bats, loikly. Hittin' the redoiy in Bremen. (*Rover walks to the bar, pours himself a drink, moves to the table and sits down beside Tabby.*)

TABBY: Dat's de truf. Yuh said a mouf'ful dere. **Ole soak! Dat han' me a laff. You'ze three sheets ta de win' yase'f.** Why dat man need ta go outta dis house fer redeye? Dem robbers lef' enuff booze in de basemin ta float de Tah-tanic. We'ze fixed fer lif'.

FAIRY TALES FOR ADULTS

ROVER: **Dat's a hot one. De rate yooz iz swillin' de stuff, de Titanic'll wind up in *dry*dock.** Well, loik we allays said back in da Bronx: ain't never been a leopard changed its spots. Dat Cocky's a city boy. Dis loif in de sticks is drivin' 'im bughouse. He's allays t'inkin' back on de time in Noo Yawk when he's singin' wopra ta all dem swells.

TABBY: Ain't no use in rakin' up ole times. We'ze comfy an' settled-in heah. An' Jen an' me, ain't we turn dis raggedy ole robber's dump inta a reg'lar home? An', ain't dem no-account, low-down hoodlums lef' all dat likker un coin behin' 'em? No use grumblin' an' grousin'. We hit de jackpot de day we skeered off dem crooks. Why sho': we kin *all* recolleck bettah times. Bes' days a ma lif' was workin' in de city for dat big exterminatin' outfit—rakin in da dough. But dem days is *long* gon'. Ain't no point in cryin' ovah milk dat's spilt on da flow.

ROVER: **I ain't never hoid such bull! Workin' for an exterminatin' outfit! Youz uz "workin'" in a cat house till ya got too ole ta toin tricks.** I bet back in dem days youz uz one hellava high-toned broad, Tab. Wish I coulda seen yuz. I wuzn't no slouch neither—in ma yoot. Had a goil in every port. Yessir—there wuz dames from Frisco ta Yokohama jus waitin' fer me ta come sailin' inta deir waitin' arms. Dem years on da briney wuz da best years a' my loif. I been roun de woild too many times ta count. I ain't called "Rover" fer nuttin'. Did I ever tell yuz dat I coulda been made a *cap*tain. Woulda—only dat sonufabitch Captain High-an'-moity queered da deal. He had it in fer me cause I'uz making' time wid da chippy he'uz fixin' ta marry.

TABBY: **Did yuh ever *tell* me! Iffin Ah had a dollah fer ever time Ah heard dat baloney, Ah'd be Rockafellah! You'as no more 'bout ta be made captain than Ah'as gonna be crowned da queen a' Englan'. You'as a hard-workin', hard-drinkin' slob uv a stoker all yur sailin' lif'.** You'd'a made a *fine* capt'in, hunny—dat fo' su'tin

ROVER: Well, 'ere's to yuz! Down de hatch! (*They clink glasses and take long draughts from their glasses.*) Ain't all our glory dies behind

91

us, Tab. Dere's loif in us yit. Why, soonaz we get our qua'tet in shape, we'll knock 'em dead in Bremen. Wunst dem city folk hears us, we'll be de tok a de town. De'll be standin' in loin, waitin' ta shell out de bucks jus ta get near us. We'll show 'em, huh Tab?

TABBY: Yuh said a mouf'ful. We ain't finish by a loooong shot. Why, soon as Old Jen starts ta feelin' bettah, we'll prak'is till we perfek. Den—watch out! Cheahs! (*They drink again. A long silence ensure, but though conversation comes to a temporary halt, their drinking does not.*)

JENNY ("OLE JEN") JACKSON *enters stage rear. She is in her eighties—an elderly, heavy-set Swedish woman with the soulful eyes and downcast expression of a tired, long-enduring donkey. Her white hair is braided and coiled atop her head in a bun. She wears a shapeless dress and an unbuttoned cardigan sweater. Assisted by a cane, she moves toward an easy chair, walking with great difficulty.*

TABBY: Why dere you iz! How yuh feelin', hun?

OLE JEN: Dese ole bones yust about reddy fer de glue fak'ory, Ay tink.

TABBY: Hush! What kinda talk's dat? Why, soonas Cocky get back heah with dat med'cin, you soon be yuh ole self. (*Tabby rises from the table and crosses to the fireplace to help Old Jen into an easy chair.*)

OLE JEN: Ay's an *ole* self—dat de troot. Ay tal you—ain't novere Ay ain't feelin' t'robby an' tvingy like. I need trink visky. Dot make me feel leedle better. Fetch me trink, Tab.

TABBY: Why sho'. Yuh jus' set dere nice an' snug, hunny. (*Tabby goes to the bar and pours Ole Jen a drink. While there, she refreshes her own.*) Here yuh be. Dat'll put de spring back in yuh step. Ah don' wanna heah no more dat talk 'bout glue fak'ories. Yuh got plenty a kick lef' in yuh yet. **Po' ole soul—coughin' ha'f de night an' moanin' dudder**

ha'f. Be lucky ta lass till fall. (*Tabby sits down in the chair opposite Old Jen.*)

ROVER: Tab's roit. It 'ud tike mor'n a few t'robs an' twinges ta croak yuz, Jen. Yu'll see de boat o' us out! **Like hell! Looks like mebbe won't be no later dan tamorrah she'll kick da bucket.** Here. Lemme light de foir fer yuz. Keep ya toes toasty. (*After crossing to the fireplace to ignite the fire, Rover returns to his chair by way of the bar, where he pours himself another drink.*)

OLE JEN: Tanks. Did visky fix me up, py yiminy.

TABBY: Das raght. Cheah up, hun. Lif's sho't, but de glass is tall! Here's to yuh!

ROVER: Mud in yur oiy!

OLE JEN: Skoal!

ROVER: Wunst yuz is back on yur pins, Jen, we'll start rehoisin' ag'in. "Sweet Adeloin" un "In de Good ole Summertoim"—all dem good ole tunes.

OLE JEN: Ve vill, py golly! "Vait till de Sun Shine, Nellie." Dot bane one svell song!

TABBY: "Kentuckah Babe." Dat's de one Ah'z pahshal to. Dat's what ma man, Tom, useta call me—his "Kentuckah Babe." Ain't never set foot in Kentuck, but dat di'n' cut no ice wid Tom. (*She laughs.*) He call me his "Kentuckah Babe" de vary night he gemme dis 'ere diamin pin an' promiss me he'z comin' back ta marry me—soonaz he made his fo'tune down deah in Souf 'Merica. Said he'z leavin' his heart wid me! (*She laughs again*) Dat old devil! Wohn Ah be on dat fam'us cloud nahn when Ah sets dese tired ole eyes on dat sweet-talkin' rascal ag'in!

OLE JEN: Dot'll be gut day, sure tang. How long Tom bane down dere in dem southern parts?

TABBY: (*Defensively*) It take *time* ta make yuh fo'tune.

OLE JEN: Vhy sure! Dat's da hones' troot, sveetie. **Dot promise ta marry ya vas false as dem daimins. Dot Tom bane gone twenty years er so. He iss no-good faller, Ay tink.**

ROVER: Why don''e wroit ya, Tab?

TABBY: Kaint write. An' besides—Ah'z been movin' roun. Don' have no permanin' address. Wheah'z he gonna write *to*—sposin' he could write? Which he kaint.

ROVER: How's 'e gonna find ya, den? How's 'e gonna know where ta come to—sposin' de guy does come back?

TABBY: (*She has no answer to Rover's question, and an awkward silence ensues. Though Rover appears to be willing enough to drop the subject, Tabby shows signs of increasing agitation. At last she erupts.*) Sposin'! Ain't no sposin' bout it! He'll be cummin' back, all raght. Don' need ta worry yur haid 'bout dat, mister! (*As Tabby takes a long drink from her glass, Rover exchanges a meaningful glance with Old Jen. Another awkward silence follows which is finally broken by Rover.*)

ROVER: Well, I'd loik ta meet dis Tom. Mus' be a hellava guy. **Fat chance yu'll see dat lyin' bum dis side a da Poily Gates. Youz uz sure one dumb boob ta fall fer dat phony faker's line.** I'll be makin' my own fortune one a' dese days. Soonaz I get de dough ta hire a schooner down ta da Caribbees. (*He pulls out a yellowed piece of paper from his shirt pocket and unfolds it. He crosses to the fireplace and, holding the paper so that the women can view it*) Ya see dis map? Got it offen an ole codger used ta skipper a tramp steamer. 'E give it ta me jus' 'fore he gave up da ghost. 'E tole where de island drawn on dis map is. An' ye see dis 'ere cross? Dat marks de spot where dere's

FAIRY TALES FOR ADULTS

treasure hidden—a big pile a' gold or sumthin'. Ain't anudder guy livin' knows nuttin' 'bout dis, 'cept me. Fie cud get down dere an' lay ma mitts on de treasure—why I cud start livin' de loif a' Roiley. I'd share da loot wid youz. Foist, dough, I gotta find a way ta get down dere.

OLE JEN: Dot nice, Rover. You got good heart. **Sometime Ay vunder vat's matter mit you! Dot map's yust plain vort'less. You show dot map so many time it got hole in it. Ay tink you got hole in da head, too.**

TABBY: Iffin dat map's sa val'able, why in de worl' di'n't dat skipper faller dig up all dat goal hisse'f?

ROVER: (*Angrily*) He 'uz meanin' to, but loik I tole ya: he croaked. An' dis map ain't no lousy fake, like youz uz allays insinuatin'.

TABBY: Ain't 'sinuatin' nuffin. Jus' wonderin'. **Lawd O Lawd—caint he'p da po' sap dat's boun' an' determin' ta fool hisse'f? We'll see dat treasure da day it start rainin' dollahs!** (*With an air of injured dignity, Rover returns the map to his pocket and walks back to his chair at the table. Behind his back Tabby and Old Jen exchange meaningful glances. As soon as Rover resumes his seat, Ole Jen beings to cough and to breath with difficulty. Alarmed, Tabby rises and stands by her side.*) Lawsy, Jen, dat hackin' an' gaspin' sound *bad!* What kin Ah do ta he'p yuh? (*She waits for the coughing fit to subside.*)

OLE JEN: Leedle more visky fix me up, Tabby. Dot visky got gut strong kick. Knock all dis cohfin' und veezin' right outa me.

TABBY: Comin' raght up, hun. (*She goes to the bar and fills both Ole Jen's glass and her own. She gives the glass to Ole Jen who takes a long swallow which, in fact, silences her cough and appears to improve her breathing.*)

OLE JEN: Tanks. (*She sighs.*) Vell, vell, da ole gray mare, she ain't vat she us'ta be!

ROVER: Arrrw, can dat, Jen! Youz uz good as ya ever wuz.

OLE JEN: Vasn't ever much, Ay'm tinkin'.

TABBY: Why hush! Weren't fer you, wheah'd we be? Who got us all tagethah—got us ta skeer dem robbers outta der wits an' outta dis house? *You.* Dat's who. Yuh wasn't no ole grey mare dat day. No suh! Nohow!

ROVER: We shore give dem t'ick-headed mugs de bum's rush! Ya kicked dem roit outta da door, din'ya Jen? 'Nd Tab, youz uz in dere a'clawin' an' a'scratchin' an' givin' dem no-'count rummies what for. I got in some good cuts maself—wid ma knoif. We fixed deir clock, huh?

TABBY: Dat's a fac'. We sholly did!

OLE JEN: Ve done gut vurk dot day. Musta been t'irdy dem bad fallers.

ROVER: Fordy, more loik.

TABBY: At lease dat. Mebbe more! It'as too dawk ta count all dem good-fer-nothin' lowlifes.

ROVER: We showed 'em! Bottom's up!

TABBY: Ah'z wid yuh!

OLE JEN: Skoal!

(*They raise their glasses and drink. A long pause ensues broken only by a resumption of Old Jen's coughing.*)

FAIRY TALES FOR ADULTS

ROVER: Well goils, never say die! Where dere's loif dere's hope. We'll show de woild yit. Couple'a rehoisals, woik out de kinks, an' our qua'tet'll be ready fer da big toim.

TABBY: Das raght!

OLE JEN: Ve vill, py yingo!

(*During the prolonged silence that ensues, Rover returns to the bar to fill his glass and Tabby does the same both for herself and for Old Jen. At last, a voice is heard off state: a man's voice singing "La Donna é mobile." The sound grows louder as the singer approaches the front door.*)

TABBY: Deah he be. At lass!

THOMAS ("COCKY") BANTAM enters through the outside door, concluding his aria with a flourish of his arms and a deep bow. He is a small man dressed in flashy clothing: a loud, plaid suit coat with a red vest; a multicolored necktie, loose at the neck; striped pants; and a red beret, which stays on his head throughout the action of the play. He has clearly been drinking and is in an expansive mood.

COCKY: Wake up, ladies and gents! Your wandering minstrel and trustworthy delivery boy has just returned from the wilds of darkest Bremen bearing soothing remedies and good tidings. Here—this is for you, Jen. (*He strides over to Old Jen's easy chair and hands her a bottle of cough syrup.*) That'll fix you up, ole darlin'. Great stuff—highly recommended by a white coat in a drug store. And here's a liquid potation that will set us all up. Champagne! Makes a change from the rotgut we usually imbibe—right Rover? (*As he continues to talk, he pops the cork on the champagne bottle, produces four glasses from the bar, and pours and distributes drinks to everyone.*) My, my, I just wish you could have seen all the rushin' about and tearin' around that's goin' on in the big metropolis. Such carryin'-on you never did see! Why hell, boys and girls, let's face it. We're getting' to be a bunch of stodgy, stick-in-the-mud hicks, sitting out here in the boondocks.

What we need is a good dose of concrete sidewalks and city lights! This dump in the woods may serve well enough as home base, but our real home—our natural *meal*-you, like the Frenchies say—is town, not country. And boy oh boy, wait till you get a load of the fancy-schmanzy fashions that the fair sex is sporting nowadays. Why Tab, they'll knock your eyes out! And Rover, believe me, you'll enjoy seeing the goods too—though knowing you, you'll be more interested in the ladies that are wearing them. Not all of'em absolutely guaranteed to be bona fide ladies. (*He laughs heartily. Rover responds with a tepid smile.*) What you two need to do is to gird your loins, leave the rural birds and the bees to their own boring devices, and join the human race. And you, Ole Jen—there'll be plenty for you to do in Bremen too. Why there's more excitement happening in one city block than there is in whole forest of trees. What have we got here to liven us up? Ooohing and aaahing over beautiful sunsets and sniffing pretty flowers. Little of that kind of pastime goes a long way, wouldn't you say, Jen? Oh, you'll have a grand time. **Look at the dumb bastards! Sitting on their kiesters all day, knocking back booze. Reliving the illustrious past and daydreaming about a glorious future. Poor suckers—soused to the gills and drunk on illusions. They're way past due for a thorough shaking-up.**

ROVER: Tanks fer da bubbly. **Dat blowhard Cocky. Allays playin' de big shot.**

OLE JEN: Ya, Cocky. I trink bubbaly now; take med'cin in leedle vile. You got good heart. **Vat iss dis med'cin! Looks like svill? Cheap snake oil, Ay betcha. Tanks fur nutting.**

TABBY: Yuh sho been gone long enuf. What yuh been doin' wid yase'f? **'Cept lappin' up hooch, Ah mean, yuh windy ole blatherskite.**

COCKY: As I said, I have tidings of great joy! You will all greatly rejoice.

FAIRY TALES FOR ADULTS

ROVER: Aw, fer Chrissake Cocky, cut de bullshit an' talk En'lish.

COCKY: Right you are, Rover, right you are. It's time we *all* stopped stalling. Time we stopped being chicken and started to talk turkey. Well, brace yourselves, my fellow vocalists. We're appearing, tomorrow night, on the stage of the Stardust Theatre. The Bremen Quartet! That's how we're being billed. It's all set up. There's no backing out now. (*All three listeners stare at him in silent disbelief.*) **Now look at 'em. Scared. I knew it. I've brought them medicine they don't want to swallow. But they'll have to. For their own good. It's nasty, sour stuff that's hard to take, but it's what the doctor ordered. They've lived with their crazy pipedreams long enough. They actually think we can sing. Sing! Our quartet sounds like a bunch of alley cats having a scrap. But they wouldn't believe it if I told them. Tomorrow, though, after we're booed off the stage and we're scraping rotten tomatoes off our shirts, they'll have to believe it. They'll have to face facts. My medicine is the cure that kills. Kills *hope*. Once they kick that deadly narcotic they can find some peace. Knowing that they can no more sing than pigs can fly, they'll have to give up all those other miserable, brainless dreams that are keeping them from resting easy in the sweet, consoling realization that they're sad, hard-luck lushes doomed to spend the rest of their lives finding whatever happiness they'll ever know at the bottom of a glass. Nobody knows better than I. I can stand up and bear reliable personal witness to the worth of my medicine. I've taken it. It made me gag, but it made me smart. It wasn't the jealousy of spiteful rivals or the greed of mercenary managers or any of that other bunk I used to try to sell to myself; it was *drink* that brought a sad end to my short career in opera. And it was hard-facts medicine that brought—finally—a happy end to my long career as a self-deceiving, wound-licking schlemiel nursing cock-eyed ambitions for a big come-back. I took the bitter medicine and I found *peace*. Of course, in my case, I *can* sing. I've proved that. But I no longer nurse any damn-fool expectation of singing opera again. A dance band crooner—maybe. The occasional spot on** one or two radio programs. That's possible. I'd have to cut back a bit on the sauce. Loose a pound or two, I guess. Practice. But first things first: I've got to throw some bright, glaring light on all this Bremen Quartet moonshine.

TABBY: Yuh loss yuh mine, Cocky! We ain't readah fer no public *day*-beyew!

ROVER: Roit. Jees, Cocky, wat wuz ya t'inkin'! We gotta rehoise.

OLE JEN: Ya. Vat Tab 'nd Rover say iss right, py golly! Ve're not reddy py long shot.

COCKY: (*Affecting astonishment*) What's this! What kind of talk is *this*! Why we've rehearsed and rehearsed till we're as good as we'll ever be.

ROVER: My troat's kinda sore.

TABBY: An' Ah ain't got nothin''propriate ta weah.

COCKY: Wear what you've got on. You look snazzy. This is a talent contest that's put on once a month. Anyone can participate. You don't even need to sign up in advance; they'll let volunteers from the audience step up on stage and do their bit. We're not talking about some ritzy, high-class affair. This event attracts hayseeds from all around the county. Why half the audience will be there in their coveralls. Now, after we win—that's different. We'll go on to New York for the semi-finals. *Then* we can think about buying some fancy outfits. And when we win there, we're off to Hollywood for the final elimination round. And if we win—and we're sure to—we'll be offered a movie contract, and we'll wind up on the silver screen!

ROVER: We ain't ready, I tell ya. Dey have dese shows ever month, why den—nex toim roun mebbe. Not tamorrah.

FAIRY TALES FOR ADULTS

TABBY: Dat's de truf! Why, iffin we prak'is ever day till . . . .

(*Old Jen is suddenly overcome with a severe coughing fit. Alarmed, she rises to her feet. Tabby and Cocky rush to her side to help her. They encourage her to sit down again. She does so and the coughing subsides, but her breathing is loud and labored throughout the rest of the action. Rover produces an afghan from the chest beneath the window, takes it to Ole Jen, and covers her feet and lap with it.*)

TABBY: Now den, yuh jes' res' yase'f a bit, hunny.

COCKY: Take it easy. Sit there a spell till you catch your breath.

ROVER: Youz uz been woikin' too hard, Jen. Yuh need some rest.

OLD JEN: (*Weakly*) Ay vill be all right. Ay res'. (*Old Jen slumps in the chair and appears to fall asleep. The other characters speak in somewhat lowered voices throughout the remainder of the play.*)

ROVER: Well, dat put da stopper on it. Ain't gonna be no qua'tet singin' tamorrah.

TABBY: No, suh. Dat's out. We'ze gonna wait till Ole Jen's feelin' bettah. Kaint have no qua'tet singin' when dey's only de three uv us. No getting' roun dat. But say, Cocky. Ah'z got it! Nothin' stoppin' *you* from showin' up at dat Starduss Theateer an' singin' solo.

COCKY: Talk sense, woman! I told the man I'd show up with a quartet. If I can't show up with a quartet, I won't show up at all!

ROVER: Why not? Dint yuz jus' say dey let anyone get up an' do deir bit?

COCKY: Don't be ridiculous! Why I haven't practiced my opera repertoire in years.

101

TABBY: What you talkin'! Why you're a'singin' dem high-class tunes *all* de time. Some ole king bellerin' about stabbin''is queen, er some fellah jus' swallered pisin an' wantin' ta sing 'bout it fer ha'f hour 'fore he croak.

COCKY: (*Angrily*) You don't know what you're talking about.

ROVER: Tab's roit! Ain't nobody readier dan *you*.

COCKY: (*With mounting agitation.*) Have either of you had extensive training in music? Does either of you know the first thing about singing? No! I'm the only one who knows something about it. I think you'll have to have the decency to grant me that. And I'm also the only one who can make an informed, in*tell*igent decision about whether I'm ready or not. So I'll thank you to mind your own business!

TABBY: Suit yase'f, hunny.

ROVER: Jees, youse'as got a prize grouch on! (*Another long silence.*)

COCKY: Aw, to hell with it! What's the matter with us?. We're out of champagne, but we're not out of liquor. Why are we sitting here like a bunch of dumb chumps looking at empty glasses? Don't try to tell me you're not thirsty, Rover. Or you, Tab. Here! What we need is to put some spirit back in the party. (*He goes to the bar, fetches a bottle of whiskey and fills everyone's glass.*) I'm not going to appear in public singing any solos. I'm part of the Bremen Quar*tet*. After we've practiced and get into shape, we'll enter that talent concert and wipe up the floor with all those other pathetic amateurs. Next month, maybe. Or the month after. Here's to us! The Bremen Quartet! (*They raise their glasses and drink.*)

ROVER: Dat's roit, Cocky. We'll show 'em!

TABBY: Yuh said a mouf'ful dere! (*Ole Jen is asleep. Tabby, Rover and Cocky are drunk and motionless. A long, long silence. The curtain falls.*)

Sweet Day of Wrath

John Steinbeck

A bright summer sun filtered through the tall oaks and dappled the ground. Busy squirrels scampered across the grass and up the trunks of tall, ancient trees, and in the cloudless sky above, jays and finches flew to and from their lofty nests. A mild, cooling breeze stirred the leaves.

At the base of a towering oak, a young girl had thrown herself prone upon the ground. Her face was buried in her hands and she was weeping. She wore a simple print dress which had survived many a washday and was embellished with several patches of assorted colors. She was barefoot.

"Cummon, Gretel-gal! What ya wanna do this-a-way fer? Ain't no pint in yammerin'. You git up, now!"

The boy who spoke these words was not much taller than his sister. He was dressed in faded blue coveralls and a thin, frayed cambric shirt. He too was barefoot.

"You hush, Hansel-Bob. I'm tar'd and hongry. Where we gonna go to? Kain't find our way back home now. Them blamed birds 'as up an' et all them crumbs I dropped 'ahind me."

"Why that's jus' nat'ral. Birds is hongry too. Ain't no mischuf in 'em."

The grieving girl was unimpressed by this reminder that human and feathered beings are akin in their needs.

DAVID R. EWBANK

"An' besides," the boy continued, "ain't nuthin' ta eat at home, any mor'n they is here. We'z jus' as good off here as we wuz back home."

"Jus' as *bad* off."

A further paroxysm of grief shook the young girl's frail frame.

"Oncet we got back home, our step-Ma'ud kick us out ag'in—like she done last time. A forest ain't no meaner 'an that ole bitch."

"Ef you're a-hankerin' and a-jibbitin' ta go off, then *go*. I say we might swell bide here as move on. Gonna die without we git some food anyways."

"I kain't go 'less you go. We're fambly. Gotta stick by each other. Now you quite bein' so skeery and mimsy-mimsy. Git on yur feet, Gretel-gal, or I'm gonna take a whang at ya. We gotta git goin'."

The boy spoke with an authority more commanding than is usual in one so young. A life of want and hardship had severely shortened the days of carefree childhood and prematurely imposed upon him adult cares and responsibilities. Responding to the stern insistence in his voice, the girl wiped away her tears.

"Where at we goin'?"

"I've been tole they's a lan' a milk an' hunny summers in this here forest. Ain't a lan', mos' likely. More like a house, mebbe, in a clearin'. A house, I guess. The way I heard it, they's plenty a grub there. Ever since bad times has hit the cuntry, they's been lots 'an lots a younguns has took off inta the forest. Took off lookin' fer sumpin' ta eat, jus' like us. Ain't nobody seen hide nur hair of 'em since. They found that house, I'm thinkin'. I'll bet ya they're there now livin' high off the hog."

"That shore sounds like a purdy place. How we gonna go 'bout gittin' there?"

"Ya see that stream over yonder? Ef we wuz ta folla that there stream, I'm thinkin' that by and by we're bound ta come up on that house. Kain't have no house lessen there's water summers near. That's how I figger her anyways."

"What ef they ain't no house?"

"Why then, they ain't."

"But, Hansel-Bob, ain't ya a-scairt?"

104

FAIRY TALES FOR ADULTS

"Nah. We'll come out awright. We're the younguns. They kain't beat us down."

The girl carefully watched her brother and, seeing that his spirit was not broken, that he had the will and the grit to keep on going, she also found within herself renewed hope and resolve. Steadying herself against the trunk of the oak, she rose to her feet.

"Now, afore we set out," the boy said, "we'd better eat sumpin'. They's a bush over there with red berries. We'd best eat a passel of 'em. Might cud be the last we'll see a food."

"How we know them berries ain't p'isin, or that they ain't gonna give us the stomickache?"

"I seen birds a-eatin' of 'em. Ef they don't kill them, likely they won't kill us neither."

The two children picked all the berries that they could reach and stuffed them into their mouths. Their hunger appeased, if not satisfied, they walked to the brink of a small stream and, cupping their hands in the crystal water, drank their fill.

"Hansel-Bob, effin we wuz ta find this milk an' hunny house, an' ef like ya wuz sayin' they's plenty a grub there, oughtn't we ta fetch some of it home ta Pa? He's starvin' too. Don't aim ta give our step-Ma nuthin' though. That damn ole wummin can starve, fer all a me."

"You watch yur tongue! We ain't let ta swear."

"Why, *you* swear. I jus' heard ya call 'er a bitch."

"That's differ'nt."

"How's cum it's differ'nt when you swear?"

Having no ready answer to this question, the boy changed the subject.

"When times git bad like they is now, a fella gits ta thinkin'. They's all this trouble and sorra that's makin' the people hongry an' mad an' mean. An' some of us, seems like, takes out our mean on one 'nuther. It's our empty bellies makes us do it. An' that ain't right, I'm thinkin'. We oughta git smart-mad, not nasty-mad. Our step-Ma—she's a bitch, that's sartin. But likely it's her empty belly that's makin' her that-a-way. But takin' food away from yur own kin—from yur own people—why that ain't no way ta act! Why, they's plenty ta go 'round.

They's rich folk ain't feelin' no pain. They's eatin' vittles and guzzlin' booze like they ain't never heard tell a mis'ry and want. I knowed a fella wuz doin' gardenin' work fer one a them well-heeled bastards that's hoggin' the fat a the land, an' that fella, he sez they's enuf food throwd away by them folks in one day ta feed his fambly fer a week. That don't make no sense. Why, there ain't no problem growin' good crops nor makin' enuf food ta go 'round—they's a problem *sharin'* it. An' I'm thinkin'—ef we wuz smart mad, not ignurant mad—why we'd see to it that they's better sharin'. Trouble is, folks like our step-Ma kain't see past the end a their noses. They get mad an' mean with their own, stead a strikin' out agin' them as won't share. We gotta get smarter, not meaner."

Having concluded his speech, the boy, embarrassed by the length and fervor of it, picked up a rock and threw in into the stream. Never before having heard her brother speak so eloquently, the girl remained silent for a long moment before remarking shyly, "Why, Hansel-Bob, the way ya talk like that, ya oughta be a minister-man."

"Aw, I ain't no hand at makin' speeches. Ain't no Bible-thumper neither. It's jus' that all this sufferin'—all the ole folks and younguns doin' without—why it get's a fella ta thinkin'. Ain't nuthin' I kin do by masef. I ain't nuthin' but a little piece a the people. But ef the people cud jine up inta one big piece, why then we cud make a noise that them rich folk ud have ta heed."

"I ain't never heard ya talk this way before. Talkin' about the people and all. Al'ays before, *we* wuz jus' the fambly. Now yur talkin' like *we* is sumpin' a lot bigger than you an' me an' Pa."

"Why it *is* bigger. Lessen we're a gonna lay back and leave all them rich sons-a-bitches run over us, we've gotta pull togither. *We* is gonna hafta start meanin' the people! An' we gonna hafta start bein' smart-mad!"

"Well," Gretel-gal said, "jus' now the only *we* is you an' me an' a whole lotta trees. Guess we'd better be movin' on."

"Tha's right. Enuf gassin'. Le's git goin'"

The two solitary children struck off deeper into the forest—two abandoned outcasts, alone and friendless. But beware, you mighty of the earth! Though they be poor and vulnerable, they are armed with

FAIRY TALES FOR ADULTS

an invisible weapon, one more powerful than a sword or a gun. They have come into the possession of an idea—an idea of brotherhood, of solidarity among the despised and neglected and downtrodden—an idea that can spread and grow in strength till it becomes powerful enough to shake the world. When people in sufficient numbers begin to speak, not of I, but of *we*, a great storm has begun to brew. Heed the still-small warning of such a seemingly negligible sign if you wish to avoid the raging tempest which it portends!

The siblings trudged on in silence. The sun had set and darkness had come to the forest when at last they stopped and determined to spend the evening beneath a towering tree. Owning nothing but their clothes, the preparations for their retirement were simple: Hansel-Bob gathered grass and moss to fashion primitive cushions for himself and his sister. There was no supper to be had, but so worn and exhausted were the two weary travelers that they scarcely noticed their hunger. They lay on the ground and within minutes, they were asleep. It was a mild summer evening, and in at least the one respect that they did not suffer from cold, nature smiled upon the abandoned waifs. They slept soundly and comfortably throughout the night.

When daylight penetrated the trees and awoke Gretel-gal, she experienced a moment of panic when she realized that she was alone. Calling his name, she rose to her feet and began to search for her brother. However, within a minute or two, he appeared, advancing toward her with such speed and determination that she sensed immediately that something important had occurred.

"Cummon, Gretel-gal! I've found her—that house I wuz tellin' ya 'bout! She's rot over yonder, not more'n a hunnert yards. I scouted aroun' and found 'er while ya slep'. That place—it's a daisy! The walls is made outta wieners and sowbelly, and the roof shingles is some kinda sanwidges. An' the door's a big ole Hershey, an' the pavin' stones leadin' to it is rock candy, an' they's a fountain. And whaddaya think's spewin' up from 'er? I took me a swig an' I'm tellin' ya twasn't no water. It uz Co'cola! An' they's a fence all aroun' the place—a funny kinda fence. It's younguns jus' our size, little gals and young fellers, and they got aholt a each other's hands. They look jus' as real and sassy as effin they uz real. But they ain't real. They uz all made outta johnnycake! An' what's more—they ain't nobody 'round the place to stop ya from eatin' all ya wanna. So cummon. Lez go."

"You sure you ain't had a dream, Hansel-Bob? This house yur talkin' 'bout—hardly seems likely such a place cud be!"

"Don' gimme no argament, gal. You cum with me!"

The house was in a clearing, just as Hansel-Bob suspected it would be. Only steps from the spot where the two had spent the night, it sparkled and gleamed in the morning sun and seemed so improbably rich and magnificent that Gretel-gal could scarcely believe in its reality. She stood transfixed at the edge of the fragrant green meadow which surrounded the fabulous cottage and gazed at it, stunned and timid. On many occasions she had stood before store windows and looked yearningly at opulent arrays of tempting merchandise which she could admire, but never hope to touch or possess. It is not surprising, then, that, seeing a house more alluring and magical than anything else she had ever encountered, it seemed to her as if a pane of glass separated her from its tempting but inaccessible abundance. But when she witnessed her brother ravenously devouring a pork chop shutter, she became convinced that the house was no mirage. She ran to his side and began to eat the door knob.

"Nibble, nibble mousie,
Who's eating my housie?"

It was a human voice—high and shrill. Startled, both children interrupted their breakfast to look about them. Seeing no one, they exchanged quizzical glances. For a moment they hesitated, as though they considered the possibility of conducting a more thorough investigation, but hunger soon got the better of curiosity and they resumed eating.

"Wizzle and wuzzle
And tit for tat,
Gobble and guzzle
Till you're full and fat.
Inside there are hotcakes
And bacon and pone.
Come in, land sakes,

Leave my house alone!"

A half chewed hunk of licorice rain gutter fell from Hansel-Bob's mouth as he stiffened in alarm and astonishment.

"Who air ya, an' where ya at?" he demanded. "I kain't see ya."

Gretel-girl, astonished at her brother's temerity, spoke to him in urgent, hushed tones.

"Shush, I tell ya. They's a sperit 'round here or sumpin'. Don't rile it up."

A strident cackling assaulted their ears. The ghastly clamor seemed to come from some source above their heads.

"Lookit, Hansel-Bob!" The terrified girl spoke in a whisper. "Up yonder, in the winda. They's a *witch*!"

"Now, now, my child. Old women have keen ears. I'm not a spirit and I'm not a witch. I'm just a poor old granny. Granny Flushpocket, that's my name. Now you two stop eatin' me out of house and home and come inside. I'll feed you a proper meal."

Within a few seconds, the front door was opened, and a wrinkled old crone, ugly and fat, beckoned her visitors inside. She had black, probing eyes and a crooked nose, and the sound of her voice was sharp and petulant. Her two uninvited visitors were too surprised and intimidated to consider disobeying the ancient granny. Even if they had not been frightened into timid submission, they were both still hungry, and their hostess, despite her repulsive appearance and forbidding manner, had promised to give them food. Quietly and without protest, they entered the cottage and, obeying the old woman's command, seated themselves at a rustic table made of hotdogs and peppermint sticks.

"Now, you sit there and don't eat the table. I'll have breakfast for ya in a jiffy."

And, true to her word, within minutes the two hungry guests were enjoying a large meal of fried eggs, grits and biscuits with molasses. Never before had they been treated to such bounty. As soon as their plates were empty, they were refilled. The famished outcasts ate till, at last, they could eat no more, and as they ate, the old witch woman, wringing her hands and sniggering, eyed them with greedy satisfaction. When they had finished, she gave a pail to

Hansel-Bob and told him to fetch water from the stream which ran at the edge of the meadow.

When he returned from his errand, Hansel-Bob found Gretel-gal standing at a sink washing dishes. The old woman was nowhere in sight. Setting the full pail on the table, he hurried to her side.

"Where at's the ole wummin?"

He spoke so softly that she was scarcely able to understand what he said, but his manner was so secretive and conspiratorial that she interrupted her work to give him her full attention.

"What gnawin' ya, boy? Speak up."

"Sssssh! Where'd she git to?"

"I dunno. She tole me ta redd up ta earn ma keep."

"Listin here. They's sumpin' mighty screwy goin' on 'round here. Did ya see how she dint eat nuthin' whilst we wuz wolfin' down all that grub?"

"Yeah. So what?"

"So she's fatter'n a pig, ain't she? What *she* eat, ya reckon? I figger she eats us kids!"

"Hansel-Bob, you tetched?"

"Keep yur voice down. Now listen. As I uz cumin' up from the stream I took a good gander at that there fence a kids that runs 'round this place. An' I'm tellin' ya, that there's the mos' pe*cul*'ar fence I ever clapped eyes on. I uz 'bout to cum on in, when all of a suddent one a them fence posts moved 'is eyes. An' I swear I heerd 'im let out a squeak—like he uz tryin to say sumpin'. Them younguns 'as had some kinda hex put on 'em, and that ole wummin is the one as has done it. You listen good to what I'm tellin' ya, Gretel-gal: she's a *witch!*"

"You gone plumb loco, boy!"

"You hush and listin! I uz standin' there givin' that johnnycake feller the once-over, an' as sure as I'm talkin' to ya, he wuz lookin' *back* at me.! Now, ya know all them childern I uz tellin' ya 'bout—them as has cum inta the woods and ain't nobody ever heard tell a what becum of 'em? They uz turned inta johnnycake—that's what becum of 'em. An' ya know why that ugly ole witch don't eat no grits nor no normal stuff? Cause she eats *kids*—that's why. She fattens 'em up and

110

FAIRY TALES FOR ADULTS

puts a spell on 'em and turns 'em inta johnnycake and eats 'em! 'An fust chanct I git I'm goin' back out there an' see effin I kin git one a them fence post kids ta talk ta me. An' mebbe I kin . . . ."

Before he could finish his sentence, he felt two heavy fists descend upon his shoulders, and he found himself in the powerful grip of the witch.

"You didn't think you could pull a fast one on old Granny Flushpockets, did you? You'd better think twice. I hear everything and know everything, and I show up when I'm least expected."

"Leave go a me!"

Hansel-Bob struggled to free himself, but his captor proved to be too strong for him.

"So, you've figured out what I'm up to, have you? Well, much good will it do you. Smart boys are just as tasty as the dumb ones. Once I've fattened you up and turned you into johnnycake, you and your sister will make fine morsels. He, he, he."

"All that food ya give us—ya wuzn't inter'sted in feedin' us hongry kids, wuz ya? You uz inter'sted in *eatin'* us! You're jus' a mean ole *witch*."

"You watch your tongue!" she snapped as she boxed Hansel-Bob's ears. "It's a dog eat dog world. It's none of my rules. It's the System! We all have to play by the rules of the System. I don't eat all the johnnycake I make. This cottage is mortgaged, and every month just as sure as shootin' I've got to pay off the bankers, and all I've got to pay 'em off with is johnnycake. And those bankers, they've got to eat too. We're all part of the System, and we've got to pay for everything we get. It's time you learned that lesson in life, you prying, snot-nosed smart aleck. Think you know everything! Well, here's something you need to know right now. There aren't any free lunches. You have to pay for everything you get. You just got a big meal. Now it's time to pay. It's only those radical troublemakers who talk about changing the System. You're not one of those, are you?"

She demonstrated that her question was rhetorical by shaking Hansel-Bob so violently that he was unable to respond, and after she had thoroughly shaken him, she pushed him into a cage and locked the door behind him. Throughout the day she continued to

DAVID R. EWBANK

provide him with liberal quantities of food; indeed, she encouraged him to eat as heartily as possible. But, knowing that her generosity was a sham, realizing that the hideous hag intended that he eat only so that he might ultimately be more edible, Hansel-Bob lost his appetite. For the first time in his short life of deprivation and want he found bleak and unattractive the prospect of eating to his heart's content.

After having observed the imprisonment of her brother, Gretel-gal could no longer doubt that what her brother had told her was the truth. By her words and behavior, the wicked woman had as much as admitted that she was a witch. Suspecting that the fate in store for her brother also awaited her, she determined to act before it was too late. Being a naturally sharp-eyed youngster, she noticed that the witch had placed the key to Hansel-Bob's cage in the pocket of her apron. In the late afternoon, as the ancient crone sat by the kitchen oven, Gretel-gal, without seeming to do so, kept careful watch on her. Comfortable and cozy in her cushioned rocking chair, the witch-woman, affected by the genial warmth of the fire, grew drowsy and, at last, nodded off. Gretel-gal, seizing the opportunity, tiptoed to her side, and as carefully and quietly as a thieving mouse, she pulled the key from the apron pocket. Within a minute she had unlocked the cage and released her brother. Indicating with a gesture that he was to remain silent and follow her out of the cottage, Gretel-gal led her brother outside.

"We gotta git. We kin run faster'n that witch. Le's go!"

"Nah, Gretel-gal. I kain't. I gotta do what I kin ta he'p them johnnycake younguns."

"What you talkin'! We gotta clear outa here. Soon as she wakes us, she'll . . . ."

"Kain't do 'er. Them hexed kids is our people. I gotta do what I kin ta he'p 'em."

Despite Gratel-gal's protests, Hansel-Bob walked to the fence and began to address it.

"Younguns! What ya standin' there dumb as posts fer? That mean ole witch uz hexed ya, but I'm tellin' ya, ya kin git shut a the hex soon as ya git ya sum backbone! Why, they's more a us than there is a her.

112

FAIRY TALES FOR ADULTS

What ya a-skairt of? She's likely got ya all cowed and daunted with all that rum-dumb talk 'bout the System, but use yur noggins, why don't ya? They ain't no System runnin' the people. System's nuthin' but people. It's *people* that's runnin' the System, an' what we gotta do is ta change the people that's runnin' it! Gotta change it so as we all git a fair shake 'stead only a few la-de-da rich fellers hoggin' everthin'. Ya ain't folks jus' ta lay down and take it, are ya? Ain't ya got more gumption and git-up than that? Ya need ta smarten up and git mad an' set about changin' things. Cummon. Don' jus' stand there. Le's git goin'!"

As he spoke, the johnnycake children came to life. At first their eyes began to shine and their faces assumed a more human aspect. Then they began to move their frozen limbs—tentatively and awkwardly at first, but soon their confidence grew, and before long they all abandoned their positions in a fixed and regimented line and stood and moved, free and independent, as live children should. Before Hansel-Bob concluded his exhortation, they were all transformed into the unique individuals that they had been before the evil magic of the selfish hag had bewitched them. Hansel-Bob and Gretel-gal recognized most of them. There were Adalou and Cissy and Sueellen and Rosy and Lulumae and Claude and Billy and Willy and Terry-Wayne. There were perhaps sixty children in all.

Hansel-Bob and Gretel-gal stared in amazement as their old friends and neighbors—playmates whose parents had long since been given them up for dead—came to life before their eyes. All of the newly humanized children turned to Hansel-Bob, the benign magician responsible for their transmogrification, and gazed at him in gratitude and admiration, waiting for him to instill within them yet more vitality—to inspire them with further purpose and exhort them to effect still more momentous change.

"Folla me!" he yelled, and leading his band of willing followers, he headed back inside the cottage. The witch, who had been awakened by the clamor outside her door, stood by her chair, her eyes wide with alarm, as an army of boys and girls surged into her house and surrounded her. Gretel-gal opened wide the oven door, and before the terrified hag quite knew what was happening to her, the children pushed her inside. With a resounding crash, the door slammed shut, and that was the last that the newly liberated children ever saw or heard of the malicious witch who, with her cunning lies, had turned them from free individuals into dumb posts.

During the next few days, the children, under Hansel-Bob's direction, dismantled the cottage, eating enough to satisfy their hunger and putting the remaining food into sacks and bags so that they could transport it back to their starving parents.

Watching the children as they cooperated with one another in their work, Hansel-Bob turned to his sister and asked, "Don't it make ya feel good ta share?"

Gretel-gal, who was sucking on a peppermint stick, nodded and smiled mysteriously.

Snow White Noir

Raymond Chandler

There's a lotta bull pitched about the life of a private dick. He's supposed to spend all his time—what time he's not chasing skirts or hitting the booze, that is—solving mysteries so complicated they'd knock Einstein for a loop. My average assignment is dull, dull, dull. Most days I'm either tailing wayward wives or twiddling my thumbs in the fly-bitten dump I call my office—waiting for a paying customer to show up—some poor schlemiel in straits desperate enough to require my humble services. It's nothing but mind-numbing, foot-flogging, routine work. And did I mention dull?

There's no money in it either. A flat *per diem* plus expenses—that's the going rate. And that's only when you're on a job. Which, take it from me, lotsa times you're not. Don't expect to make a fortune sleuthing. You'll be lucky to make ends meet. Many's the time my wallet's been as bare as Ma Hubbard's pantry.

So, seeing as how my professional life's no spring picnic, I may be excused for thinking that things had taken a definite turn for the better when, a few weeks back, I was called to the palace by the Wicked Queen. Now there's a broad who's loaded. Her little *pied à terre* is so up-scale and spread-out it woulda made the Bourbons of Versailles sigh. (And speaking of them, I can report first-hand that there's plenty of bourbon available at the queen's digs. I wouldn't go so far as to call her a lush, but that dame can really lap up the sauce. She's developed a yen for raw rye, and she's not one for half measures. But, give her her due, she's not stingy; she pours potables for guests as liberally as she treats herself.) I was more than grateful to be a prospective employee on the payroll of such a flush client. Finally, I thought, a chance to put a little pep back into my puny bank balance.

So there I was—hauling my weary carcass up about a hundred marble steps and ringing a bell at the queen's door, a golden portal so big and flashy it could be sited from outer space. Then I was left to cool my heels, waiting with ill-simulated patience for Her Highness to admit My Lowliness. Five minutes or so after my third ring a liveried lackey appeared—a bulky, brawny brute. He looked down his broken nose at me.

"You rang?"

This sour-faced mutt acted like he was King of the Hill. I reckoned he needed to be taken down a peg or two.

"Three times, mac. Ya deaf?"

"What?"

Turned out the guy's deaf.

I had to yell at him to get it into his skull that I had an appointment with the Wicked Queen. He finally got the picture, and I went traipsing after him through one parlor after another, each one fancier than the last, only to be turned over to another bruiser in livery—this one sporting a pair a shades and leaning on a cane.

"You here to see the Wicked Queen?"

"I'm not in Cleveland, bud. And these are the queen's digs, aren't they? Ya blind?"

"Wise guy, huh? Just keep your fat trap shut and follow me."

And we're off. Tap, tap tap—the cane leading the way.

Turned out the guy's blind.

So—another trek through some more snazzy salons that looked like no one ever kicked off his shoes and relaxed in em. And again I was handed over to yet another lackey. This palooka was something else. Shoulders as broad as a football field, and a mug that would

FAIRY TALES FOR ADULTS

stop clocks. He looked me over as though he was sizing me up for his supper.

"Hi, Tiny. Is there another flunky half a mile down the road or is there some chance I might someday get to clap eyes on her Wickedness?"

He gave me an icy, threatening glare and made a clumsy, lumbering move like he was thinking about throwing a punch in my gut. I flicked back my trench coat, quick, and put my hand of the iron I was wearing. Didn't draw. Didn't need to. A little peek of my weaponry was deterrent enough. He froze.

"What's the matter. Gat got your tongue?"

No answer.

Turned out the guy's dumb.

Pun intended.

Making sure my escort was always a couple paces ahead of me where I could keep an eye on him, we went through yet another set of doors and entered, finally, the queen's chambers. A regular Hall of Mirrors. There were enough reflections in that joint to make a guy dizzy. Everywhere I looked there were hundreds of me. The back of my head. The front. Right and left profile. It was exactly the kind a place where artsy film directors like to stage the final shoot-out so that about a dozen mirrors get shattered before the villain gets his.

I was so busy sorting out me from my duplications that at first I didn't see her. But there—hidden behind a fog bank of cigarette smoke, lounging lasciviously on a gilded chaise longue—was the Wicked Queen herself. In the flesh.

And what flesh! And what a lot of it! If her décolletage had been any deeper, she would have needed suspenders.

"That will be all, Bruno."

Bruno, the bruiser, bowed and retreated to the door. *To* it, not out of it. He stood a few yards off, silent and stolid, casting a malignant eye on yours truly.

"You mustn't let Bruno bother you. He's one of my bodyguards."

"A pretty lot a goons ya got guarding the place, Queen. They look like alumni of Sing Sing."

"Singing is the one think I can count on them *not* to do. Discretion and loyalty are the chief traits I require in an employee. My guards are a rough lot, sure, but they suit me."

"Hear no evil, see no evil, speak no evil, huh? Those apes are just the ticket for a Wicked Queen."

"You're quick, dick."

I nodded in agreement

It didn't take eyeglasses to see right off that this bird was trouble, but if a shamus avoided trouble, he'd soon be unemployed.

"Well, before we talk about this gig I've got you in mind for, let's get down to business. Name your poison."

"Whiskey, when it's available."

"Almost everything in this palace is available."

She shot me a sultry, knowing look and rose to her feet. Slipped and swayed to her feet is more like it. That dame couldn't make a motion without bringing *every*thing into play. And any man who wouldn't want to romp in her playpen would have to be either gone in the noggin or gone to glory.

She slunk over to the swankiest wet bar outside Vegas and selects one from about a hundred bottles.

"How'll ya have it?"

"As quick as possible, sugar. And neat."

She filled two glasses and handed me one.

"Here's how," she said.

"Down the hatch," I replied.

Man! That brew was smoother than a baby's butt. Nothing at all like the rotgut I'm used to imbibing.

"Well now, you act like someone who's been around the block a couple a times. Would you describe yourself as a man who's discreet and loyal?"

"Don't have much occasion to describe myself. I leave that to the next guy."

"A few of the guys I've talked to say you're . . . reliable."

She chose that word carefully, as though she were avoiding a more appropriate, but less tactful alternatives. Like *broke*.

"I strive to please."

FAIRY TALES FOR ADULTS

"Well here's my proposition. File it under 'missing person's case.' I've got this stepdaughter. Cute little thing, in her way. Chirpy and cheery." (Was it my imagination, or did "chirpy and cheery" sound like "irksome and irritating"?) "The poor dear's got herself lost. Went walking in the woods a while back and simply vanished. And I'd like to find her. If you help me locate her, I'm prepared to pay you . . . ."

And she mentioned a figure that was even more attractive than her own.

"Would that sum be agreeable?"

I was going for a nonchalant pose, and I would have handled it more suavely if the dough she was offering hadn't brought on such a coughing fit that booze was coming out my nose.

"You're more than fair, Your Munificence," I stammered.

"You better believe it, buster. I'm the fairest in the land."

And then she did a funny thing. She looked at herself in one of her mirrors, but instead of being pleased by the view, she gave me the wacky notion that she had a grudge against the *mirror*.

"Just one thing. I want this little project to be carried out strictly on the Q.T. Can you keep it under wraps?"

"For the royal price you named, Queen, my lips are as sealed at Tut's tomb."

Of course I knew right off something about her story was fishy. Why would a Wicked Queen want to know the whereabouts of a chirpy little chit unless there was some evil at the bottom of it? And why be so hush-hush if her motive was strictly legit? But at least *prima facie* the job seemed to be on the up-and-up. And anyway, I needed the dough.

"I'll take the case," I said. "What's this doll's name?"

"Snow White. That's a clue. Don't go looking for her in any tanning parlor. And remember, keep this under your hat. I have ways of rewarding loyal service, or . . . ." She cast a significant glance at Bruno. "Well, let's just I have ways of *not* rewarding rats."

"My, my! *Rat*'s a hard word, sweetheart."

"Maybe, but I always believe in calling a spade a spade."

"Yeah? Well, I'm not a rat, and my name's not Spade. You can call me Phil."

119

"I'll expect you to call on *me*, Phil. Just as soon as you discover the whereabouts of the silly little cun . . . . er, cunning little darling. You know where to find me. I'm already looking forward to our next *tête-à-tête*." She gave me a long, lingering look. "Till then."

That devious dame sure knew how to light a guy's fire with a smoldering glance. One of the facts of life generally skipped over in Sunday school is that a flame burns with the same heat whether it's lit by a saint or a sinner.

"Ta ta, toots. An a ta to you too, Bruno. Enjoyed your company." That hulking gorilla grunted and glowered.

No sense of humor.

Well, truth to tell, what smarts I've got are of the street variety. On the mean boulevards and byways of the concrete jungle I'm in touch with my primal instincts and my private sources: urban savants like Mike ("the Mule") McGukin, Cy ("Nosey") Stankowitz, and Sal ("Slippery Heels) Hunniker. I didn't cotton to the idea of finding some albino bimbo who'd managed to lose herself in the boonies. I'm as lost in the woods as the proverbial innocent babe. The forest is a big, dark place, and there isn't a friendly neighborhood bar on every corner. There aren't any corners either. Just hills, and trees and bugs. I discovered that about a billion or so itty-bitty winged critters hang out in the woods—each one hungrier for blood that Al Capone.

But, to look on the bright side, though the woods are full of deer and bears and squirrels and bugs, not many members of the human species are dumb enough to locate there, and those that do stick out. I was only a few hours on the job when I heard what sounded like a gang of men making like a chorus of Carusos. So I concealed myself behind a sturdy oak and, pretty soon, caught sight of seven Munchkins marching Indian-file down a dusty path, happy as Bingo. So, I decided to tail em to see where they were headed. After a mile or so they led me to a rustic little Swiss chalet in a sunlit clearing which they entered without knocking. Obviously, they had found their way home.

I sneaked up to the window for a look-see. And whaddaya think? There, standing at the head of a long wooden table stood this simpering chick with a milky complexion, dishing out supper to the

FAIRY TALES FOR ADULTS

little runts. She was not a bad looker, if you like that type—pure as the driven snow and twice as bland.

And the shrimpy guys she was serving—they were a batch of loonies if ever I saw em. One kept sneezing all over the food. Another nodded off in his soup, and this one genius kept getting all tangled up in a droopy shirt that was about three sized too big for him. What a dope!

But Snow White seemed to be just as content as a bee in a jam pot. For a doll who'd been brought up amid all the pampering luxury of a palace, this rustic hideaway seemed to suit her to a T. She was very happy and carefree. Very animated.

I hung around for a few days, casing the joint. I figured these woodland midgets might be up to something shady—fencing hot loot or peddling coke or, maybe, holding Whitey for ransom. Boy was I ever barking up the wrong theory! Nobody ever came near the joint. Mornings, the little guys went singing off to work; evenings, back they came, all chipper and a capella. Between times the Wicked Queen's stepdaughter happily busied herself with domestic chores, helped by a cooperative cohort of adorable birdies and beasties. If Snow White was lost and pining for home, she certainly put up a good front.

Well, I returned to the palace, reported what I'd discovered and pocketed my princely fee.

But something kept eating at me. Why was the bug I'd put in the queen's ear such a hot scoop that she was willing to shell out a small fortune for it?

It was none of my business, of course. I'd done a job and collected my pay. The end. The smart thing to do would be to let it go. But I couldn't. Let's just say that I don't like being played for a sap. I couldn't help thinking that since Her Royal Wickedness was obviously up to no good, I had been used as her unwitting instrument. I made up my mind to conduct a further, unremunerated investigation into the matter.

I know, I know. Curiosity killed the cat. Mind your own business. Leave well enough alone. Maybe it's just that what the average Joe calls "well enough" isn't good enough for me.

So, a day or so later, there I was, lying low in some bushes, checking the dwarf's domicile to see if Whitey was still as safe and deliriously happy as she was the last time I'd laid eyes on her. And after about an hour of slaughtering bugs and fighting back brambles, what do I see but this wizened old witch, all hunched over and cackling a mile a minute, making her way to the front door. With the hand that wasn't holding the largest, reddest apple I've ever seen, she knocked.

It took me only a fraction of a split second to tumble to this lame gambit. What are the odds that some slap-happy hag would be selling fruit door to door in the middle of a forest where one door is about fifty miles distant from the next? If that Halloween fright isn't really the Wicked queen, I said to myself, I'll eat my fedora.

But I couldn't bank on Whitey's not being suckered by the disguise. She was sugar and spice and everything nice, but, let's face it, more than a little bit simple. I decided that the poor frail was in need of a quick-thinking protector and that I was the only available candidate. But just as I stepped forward to put my noble resolve into action, a blackjack smacked into my cranium and sent me off to tweet tweet land.

When I came to, who knows how much later, who did I see, swimming through the mist, but Bruno. He was holding a Lugar so close to my puss that the barrel looked like Big Bertha.

"Tsk, tsk, Bruno. Did your mother never tell you that it's not nice to go around coldcocking your fellow citizens?"

A brief, feral grunt was his only response.

"What's that? You say your mother was a pig?"

As a general rule, insulting a slow-witted, hot-tempered goon who's holding a gun on you is not a smart tactic. But I was running no risk. I had such a close-up view of that rod I could see that the safety was on.

Bruno turned red in the face, pulled the trigger, and looked as surprised and disappointed as the naughty little lad who found a dog turd in his Christmas sock. While he was doing a slow double take, I knocked the gun out of his hand, got back on my pins, whipped our my Colt and planted two bullets in the dumb lug's belly. Then I was off and running to the homunculi's habitat—my head throbbing like a derelict flivver, a lump on my noggin the size of Dempsey's fist.

But I was too late. Whitey had already bitten the apple and the dust. Her midget hosts had knocked off work and were grieving over her prostrate body.

"Where did she get to?" I asked them. "The cackling crone?"

One grumpy old guy pointed to a crag that beetled over the valley. Storm clouds had gathered and reduced visibility, but I could just make out the queen in her witch's outfit, making her get-away over the mountain.

I might never have caught up with the homicidal hag if she hadn't miscalculated her escape route and wound up in a rocky cul-de-sac. The rain was pouring buckets when I finally cornered her—soaking wet but still as feisty and fierce as a Bengal tigress.

"You!" she hissed.

"The same," I said, panting from the climb.

"Phil, don't be hasty. Put your piece back in your pocket. You wouldn't plug a lady, would you?"

"Where is she? Don't see one."

"Phil, honey, stop and think. Just as soon as I throw off this dreary disguise and swallow a potion, I'll be as sexy and desirable as before. I took a shine to you the first time I laid eyes on you, you big, handsome brute. I'd like to prove to you how grateful a Wicked Queen can be.

"Grab air, sister, and can the sweet talk. I'm taking you in. You'll be booked for murder."

"Never!"

Hatred flared in her eyes as she reached under her cape for her weapon. I fired three times and she fell, screaming in impotent fury.

It was a long way down to the valley floor. I could barely hear the squishy thud as she landed.

Well that was the end of that caper. My brief brush with royalty.

The rags got it all wrong, as usual. "Accidental death" was the official story. The coroner and the coppers knew better, naturally. Three bullets are no accident, but no one could ever pin the rap on me.

And, oh yeah. Snow White—she didn't croak after all. Some good-looking young kid gave her mouth to mouth resuscitation. When she came to, he fell for her and they got hitched. I never met the guy, but Molly Givens, friend of mine who works at City Hall, met him when he and Whitey applied for the wedding license. She said he was a prince of a fellow. Charming.

Beauty and Beastski

Tennessee Williams

Characters

Beauty

A sprightly, attractive woman of indeterminate age—neither young nor quite middle-aged. In both manner and appearance she gives the impression of a practiced and accomplished flirt, desperately holding onto her implacably receding youth. A muted but unmistakable hint of hysteria underlies her gay, light-hearted banter. Nevertheless, she is a strong-willed, determined woman.

Beastski

A man who might be described as handsome were it not for the fact that he has abandoned all pretense of civilized decorum. He is unshaven, unkempt and unwashed. Nevertheless, he exudes raw animal magnetism in his every word and gesture.

Pedestrians

Scene

The interior of a large hall. Though the room is richly appointed, evidence of neglect is everywhere to be seen. Empty beer cans litter the floor. The window drapes are torn and ripped from their hangers.

DAVID R. EWBANK

Unwashed dishes and scraps of food cover a banquet table in the center of the room. On a gilded settee, downstage right, lies a pile of discarded clothing. In short, a palatial bachelor pad.

The hall is not a setting for a straightforward realistic drama that unfolds amid painstakingly authentic décor. The play is poetic. Above the hall is a screen on which is projected the image of a rose with thorns. The rose symbolizes beauty. The thorns symbolize danger. The image symbolizes dangerous beauty. Music appropriate to the mood of the action issues from an unknown source. On the street outside the fourth invisible wall pedestrians stroll by, enhancing and emphasizing the emotional tone of the action.

Act One

[*Beauty enters through large door stage left. Dressed in a light summer frock, she wears a cape around her shoulders and carries a purse.*]

BEAUTY: Yoo hoo! [*She stands uncertainly by the door*] Ah say, 'Yoo hoo!' [*There is no answer. Hesitantly, she turns and shuts the door.*] Anyone home? [*Eliciting no response, she moves toward the table and stands still, examining the room. Evidently astonished and dismayed by what she sees, she removes her cape and places it on the one of the banquet table chairs.*] Mah, mah! It's simply *shockin'* the conditions a man's content to live in. It would require the descriptive powers of Mr. Charles Dickens to capture the squalor of such a sorry sight. This scene of devastation is a veritable *bleak* house. [*Seeing a mirror hanging by the door through which she entered, she walks over to it and examines her face*] Oh mah goodness! Ah'm in urgent need of some restorative repairs mahself. [*She removes a comb and compact from her purse, combs her hair, applies lipstick, and powders her face.*] Theah. That's bettah. First impressions are *so* important. [*She returns to the table and places her purse on chair next to her cape.*] Gracious, this table simply cries out for a woman's attentions! [*She begins to tidy the table, stacking dishes and wiping the surface with a soiled napkin. Her housekeeping efforts are cut short by an ear-shattering roar. She screams, looks about her and discovers Beastski, who has been in the room all*

FAIRY TALES FOR ADULTS

along. He is standing in a dark corner by the window, partially hidden by a life-sized statue of a satyr.]

BEASTSKI: Waderya doin'? Leave my stuff be!

BEAUTY: Sir! What can you be thinkin'—frightenin' a poor, unoffendin' lady half out of her *wits*? And all because Ah was atttemptin' to tidy up the tiniest little bit.

BEASTKI: Who axed ya?

BEAUTY: Why no one *asked* me. Ah was moved by the pure spirit of charity—tryin' to help mah fellow man.

BEASTSKI: Oh yeah? I know you. I've been expectin' ya. I got this buddy sells plumbing equipmin. His travels take him to your neck of the woods. He put a bug in my ear: told me yur real good at helpin' yur fellow man—and that yuh aint too choosy about what men either. [*A saxophone wails "Red Hot Mamma."*]

BEAUTY: Slander! Mean-spirited, small-minded slander. [*Regretting this spontaneous outburst, she collects herself and replies with offended dignity*] Ah'm sure Ah don't know what you mean.

BEASTFKI: Sure, sure.

BEAUTY: Ah've come here to *clar*ify what Ah'm just sure must be a misunderstandin' between you and mah daddy. He informed me that you became perfectly *fur*ious with him, and all because of a little ole rose. When he said you became murderously irate over such a trifle, Ah simply could not believe that such a thing could be. Ah said to mahself, Ah said there must be a failure of communi*ca*tion heah. Ah said, Ah just *know* that the kind man who fed mah daddy, who proffered succor and shelter, like the good Samaritan Ah'm sure he is, could not work himself into a rage over something so slight as one single, solitary rose. And now Ah'm actually heah in your presence, why Ah can just *see* that you're not the sort of person who could be so petty and vindictive. Why, Ah saw as Ah was enterin' that you have an entire garden of roses. Surely you cannot begrudge mah daddy a rose—one he picked, not for himself, but solely and entirely to pleasure me. Mah daddy is *such* a gentleman. Never a thought for himself. If ever a true Christian walked the face of this sad ole earth, that Christian is mah sainted daddy. And to *think* that he should forfeit his precious life over such a triflin' matter . . . . Why, Ah said, Ah will just pay a visit to mah daddy's rose-growin' host and *clar*ify.

BEASTSKI: We gotta law. The Lex Talionis. An eye for an eye; a life for a rose.

BEAUTY: What a perfectly *silly* law! What earthly good would takin' a life do? That can't bring back the rose—which, I might add, lasted only one brief, glorious day before it shriveled and died. [*Strains from an orchestral version of "Le Spectre de la Rose" swell to a climax*]

BEASTSKI: Da law's da law, toots.

BEAUTY: Ah simply re*fuse* to accept it. Now look heah. Why don't you just come right on out of that corner you're lurkin' in. That's right. Now you sit down theah. Yes. And Ah'll sit heah, and we'll have a friendly little chat. Pretty soon we'll be seein' eye *to* eye. No more of this eye *for* an eye nonsense. [*Reluctantly, Beastski walks to a chair and sits down.*] Now, sir, it is crystal cleah to me that you need a woman to take charge of this place. [*Beastski groans*] Hear me out! Mustn't grumble before we're stung, must we? That's what mah daddy always taught me. I want you to listen, patiently and carefully, to mah proposal. Don't go rejectin' it out of hand. I've spent many an hour workin' it out, and many a weary hour makin' mah way heah to present it to you. I had *such* a lot of bother getting heah. Ah took a omnibus called Dalliance which took me down Primrose Path, past Paradise Garden, till, at long last, Ah arrived at your imposin' manor—Grande Étable. And *mah* am Ah parched! Mah throat's

FAIRY TALES FOR ADULTS

as dry as the Sa*harah*! Ah could certainly put a lovely cold drink to good advantage. Would you happen to have some liquid refreshment you could spare a poor wiltin' wayfarer?

BEASTSKI: [*Pointing to a carafe of water on the table.*] Help yurself.

BEAUTY: [*Looking at the table, she considers withdrawing her request, but upon second thought, changes her mind.*] You wouldn't happen to have a clean glass?

BEASTSKI: Yeah. [*He reaches for a glass, half full of water, and pours its contents into another glass. Then, using a corner of a handy napkin, he wipes out the glass and hands it to Beauty.*]

BEAUTY: [*gamely*] Well, when in Rome! [*She pours water from the carafe into her glass. Then, removing a flask from her purse, she adds a healthy shot of bourbon to the water.*] Purely for disinfectant purposes, you understand. [*Beasksti does not reply. He watches, cynically grinning, as she downs half the drink in one draught.*] That's bettah! Much, much bettah. Now—to resume. As Ah was sayin', finally, after much trouble and travail I arrived at your lovely home and . . . . Well sir—forgive me for bein' blunt—but—the unmistakable fact is that your domicile has been sadly neglected. Just look about. Why, within a week I could turn this house into a *home.* [*A jazz combo plays a few measures of "There'll Be Some Changes Made."*]

BEASTSKI: It's *my* house, sister. And don't you forget it.

BEAUTY: For*get* it! Why, how could Ah? Ah've come heah out of the goodness of mah heart to *help* you. I ask nothing for mahself. [*A milkman comes by. He is wearing a shirt on the back of which appear the words 'Human Kindness Dairy.' He leaves a bottle of milk by the front door and walks off stage.*] Of course, I do want you to drop this preposterous fixation you have developed—takin' a life for a rose. Why, the very idea!

129

DAVID R. EWBANK

BEASTSKI: Aint my idea, lady. Da law's da law.

BEAUTY: [*Placing the fingers of one hand on Beastski's knee*] Forgive me, sir, but when you talk like that, do you know what you put me in mind of? A parrot—that's what. An old parrot bird we had when I was a little girl. That bird—he would cock his bright green head and repeat what anyone said to him—just as quick and pert. And he never had the least idea what he was sayin'. It was all just meanin'less gibberish to him. But to look at that sassy ole bird and listen to his chatter, why—if you didn't know better—you might think he believed he was sayin' something important.

BEASTSKI: [*angry*] Where do you get off callin' me a parrot? What are you? A mockinbird?

BEAUTY: [*laughing girlishly*] That's *right*! Why, sir, you are a *poet*! Beneath that grease stained undershirt you're wearin' there beats the heart of a genuine poet. I am indeed a mockin' bird. That's just what Ah am doin'—mockin' you. Ah'm appealin' to your bettah nachur.

BEASTSKI: Oh yeah? I know a thing or two about nature, sweetheart. Ya wanna be careful when you start appealin' to nature. [*The beat of jungle drums, scarcely audible at first, increases in volume and intensity till the end of the act.*]

BEAUTY: [*apprehensive*] It is your *bet*tah nachur Ah am appealin' to.

BEASTSKI: I've never had no complaints. My wimmen never had nature better than they had it with me. [*He stands up and rips off his undershirt.*]

BEAUTY: [*Determined to maintain a light, bantering tone.*] Sir, you have a most im*pos*in' physique. Why, a fine, strong gentleman like yourself—a poet at heart—must do a lot a good in the world—defendin' the weak and the needy. [*Her chatter becomes more hysterical as she becomes more alarmed.*] Ah'm sure we can come to some *am*iable agreement about this rose business. If amends are what you are demandin', why Ah'm more than willin' to make whatever amends I can for mah daddy's innocent, *blame*less act. As Ah say, Ah could turn this sty—I mean—stylish residence, which you have unfortunately permitted to suffer a sad decline, into the nice, cozy little nest. Ah've had years of experience in domestic management.

BEASTSKI: How many year's, Beauty? How old are yuh?

BEAUTY: Sir! A gentleman never inquires after a lady's age.

BEASTSKI: Yeah? Well, I'm inquirin'. You've been around the block more than once, sweetheart. Yuh can't fool me with all yur fancy schmanzy talk. I've got this buddy sells sewin' machines . . . .

BEAUTY: Stop! [*Polishing off her drink, she stands and defiantly faces Beastski*] Why shouldn't *Ah* have a chance *live*! What could you possibly know about me? Existin' under the same roof with two vindictive, selfish, ugly sisters. Always scrimpin' and savin'—makin' do with the measly means mah poor daddy could provide. Ah grew *weary*! Weary, Ah tell you. So Ah reached out to grasp some shred of beauty, of love—of *life*—before it was too late—before life passed me by—like some omnibus that goes whizzing by and nevah stops to let *me* get on. Ah got tired to mah bones of the prose of life. Who can blame me if Ah reached out to grasp some *poetry*!

BEASTSKI: Poetry, huh? Let's me and you make some poetry right here! [*He lunges forward and roughly embraces Beauty, who screams, feebly and unconvincingly. The lights in the hall grow dim, and a spotlight falls on a withered old crone who walks across the stage selling flowers and calling out: "Flowers. Flowers. Don't delay. Gather ye rosebuds while ye may. No one's getting any younger. Flowers. Get your flowers here."*]

[*Curtain.*]

DAVID R. EWBANK

Act Two

Six weeks later. The hall is completely transformed. There are no beer cans on the floor; there is no discarded clothing on the furniture, and no unwashed dishes litter the tabletop. The room is clean, well-polished and tidy. The torn drapes have been replaced by chintz curtains. On various surfaces about the room there are vases holding freshly cut flowers. A large photograph of Beauty and Beastski as bride and groom hangs on the back wall. Embroidered antimacassars are pinned to every chair and to the settee. A framed work of handicraft, cross-stitched letters spelling "Home Sweet Home," hangs on the wall by the entrance. There are colorful rag rugs on the floor. The life-sized statue of a satyr has been removed. The screen image of a rose with thorns remains unchanged.

[*Beauty enters through large doors stage left. She wears a light summer frock and a sunbonnet. In one hand she carries a pair of shears, and in the other, a large bouquet of red roses. She places the roses in an empty vase atop a sideboard situated under the mirror and puts the shears in the top drawer of the sideboard. She removes her bonnet and puts it next to the vase. Then, after carefully arranging the flowers, she examines herself in the mirror, adjusts her hair, and turns to face the room.*]

BEAUTY: Yoo hoo! Darlin'! [*There is no response.*] Yoo hoo. [*She looks in the direction of a door stage right.*] Come out, come out wherevah you are. [*Still no response.*] He must be hidin' out in that "study" of his. Ah declare, Ah don't know *what* he gets up to in theah. He's not studyin'—that's a certainty. Ah am never able to detect any evidence that he spends his time improvin' his mind. No one could honestly say his conversation scintillates with choice *bon mots* and clevah witticisms. Quite the contrary indeed. For hours on end Ah can scarcely wheedle a word out of him. [*She giggles.*] Oh well. Poor deah. If he wants to sulk in his den like an ole hibernatin' beah—Ah will not interfeah. That "study" may remain off limits to me, so long as the rest on the house is *mah* domain.

132

FAIRY TALES FOR ADULTS

[*Beastski opens the study door and enters. He is as transformed as the hall. He is clean-shaven, his hair is combed, and he is dressed in suit pants, a long-sleeved dress shirt and well-polished black shoes.*]

Oh, theah you are. My don't you look like a fine gentleman in your new suit! But remember now, before my daddy and sisters arrive, Ah'm expectin' you to put on a coat and tie. First impressions are *so* important. [*An organ rendition of "There's No Place Like Home" is heard in the background. It becomes increasingly frenzied and dissonant as Beauty speaks. A young man dressed as a sailor strolls across the stage wearing a sandwich board: "Join the Navy: See the World."*] Ah know Ah shall nevah forget mah first impression of *you!* [*Beauty laughs. Beastski walks to the settee, sits down, and prepares to light a cigarette.*]

Sweetie! How many times have Ah told you: when you want to indulge in your nasty habit of inhalin' foul tobacco fumes, either retreat to your study or go outside. That nasty smoke gives me a splittin' headache. And you keep forgettin' that Ah've moved all the ashtrays out of this room. Nothin' is more un*sight*ly that a collection of ugly ole cigarette butts. [*Beastski returns the pack of cigarettes to his shirt pocket. Looking downcast and discouraged, he assumes a recumbent position of the settee, resting his head on one of the upholstered arms and kicking his feet up onto the seat of the settee.*] That's right, deah. You take a little nap before our guests arrive. But you *know* Ah don't want you getting' your shoes on that lovely upholstery. Why, within weeks it will begin to look worn and threadbeah. You take your shoes off, now. Ah've told you and told you. [*Resignedly, Beastski puts his feet on the floor.*] And you should know by now how badly hair oil stains fabric. My sweet little antimacassars, which Ah painstakingly made with mah own two hands, provide *some* protection, but if you must lie down theah, allow me provide you with a towel to put under your head. [*Beastski resumes a sitting position, refusing her proffered assistance with a wave of his hand.*]

Isn't it excitin'—mah family movin' in today! Won't mah two sisters turn positively green with envy once they discovah their long-sufferin'

133

DAVID R. EWBANK

sister livin' in such luxury? And when they see the size of this weddin' ring! Why, this stone alone will pay them back for years of their sneerin' condescension. And my dear daddy—if anyone deserves some peace and tranquility in his declinin' yeahs, surely it's that dear, lovin', *saintly* man. Why darlin', you won't hardly notice his presence, he's so quiet and self-effacin'. And as for my sisters. Well, Ah've been meanin' to talk to you about them. If mah plans work out, we won't have to put up with them for long. Ah've been hatchin' schemes in this busy ole head of mine, but— if mah schemin' is to have the least chance of succeedin', Ah require your cooperation. Ah'm sure you have some lovely gentlemen friends to whom we could introduce Drucilla and Hortense. We could invite them ovah for a party. They needn't be anybody special. Middle-aged widowers will do. Mah sisters are in no position to be choosy. Indeed, Ah believe Ah may assure you that they would both accept the proposal of any man who offered. Won't you help me arrange that, sweetie? Oh not right away—but soon. Ah do not relish the idea of livin' under the same roof with mah two sisters for the rest of mah life. Now deah, you just sit theah and com*pose* yourself while Ah nip upstairs and change into somethin' more allurin'. Mustn't look like a dowdy old Hausfrau when mah family arrives, must Ah?

[*Beauty exits by a door upstage right. As soon as the door shuts, Beastski springs up and disappears into his study. Moments later he returns carrying a dufflebag on his shoulder. He is smoking a cigarette. Placing a note on the table, he walks to a "window" in the invisible fourth wall, puts two fingers in his mouth and whistles. The sailor with the sandwich board reappears. Beastski indicates that the sailor is to wait for him. Before exiting by the front door, Beastski removes the cigarette from his mouth and grinds it out on the floor. He joins the sailor and both hurry off stage. Moments later, Beauty, wearing a peignoir, rushes in.*]

Whatevah in the world was that ear-shatterin' noise! [*She looks around the empty room.*] Why, what's this? [*Seeing the note on the table, she picks it up and reads it.*] "Ah'm off the see the world. Don't wait up." Well, Ah declare! [*She runs to the "window" in the fourth wall*

FAIRY TALES FOR ADULTS

and looks up and down the street. Seeing nothing, she goes to the front door, opens it and looks out. Nothing. As she shuts the door, she notices the cigarette on the floor and emits a shriek of dismay.] Why, what a mean, vindictive thing to do! [*She stoops to pick up the cigarette.*] Oh well! [*She straightens her shoulders and adopts a defiant pose.*] Now mah home is really mah *own*! Who needs a man? Men are *beastly* creatures!

[*Curtain.*]

136

The Old Gingerbread Man

Ernest Hemingway

He was an old man and he was made of gingerbread. He was poor. He came from Hell's Kitchen and all his life had had been a runner. He had not been sorry to run away from his home where food was always scarce. He had not been lucky. He had never known the happiness of those who have real homes. But what is luck, he thought. Those who are lucky today will be unlucky tomorrow. He had strong legs and good wind. Was that not luck of a sort—a poor man's luck? And if he had not been lucky in other ways, well then, he thought, he must substitute grit for luck.

He had run well. Again and again he had outrun rivals. He had always been a winner. He was old now, but he was still the undisputed champion. In the beginning it had been easy. The jeering threshers, his first competitors, had run on conceit and bluster, and that had dried up and done them in before he had even begun to tire. In those days he was never troubled by doubt. He counted upon his own strength as a man relies upon the coming of dawn. No force could hold it back. No calamity could thwart it. Now his legs were old and his breath came with difficulty. But not always with difficulty. He was often good for miles before the bitter coppery taste came into his mouth and he began to feel a pain in his lungs like the pricking of a small sharp knife. A slight pain, at first—a pain that a man might almost imagine that he imagined. But then, later, as the race wore on, the pain grew and demanded that it be noticed. In the old days, he had contended against runners; now, more and more, he struggled with himself. He fought the weakness of his body and he fought the insidious doubts which infiltrated his mind and sapped his confidence like a sinister fifth column.

He was out on the road now and the late afternoon sun cast long shadows. A mild September breeze coming from the northwest ruffled the grass along the roadside and bathed his face. He felt fit and alert. He was by himself now, but he knew that that was bound to change. He had often done without food or rest, but never had he gone for long without competitors. Them he could count on. They came as surely as old age and death. Well, let them come, he thought. He felt fit and ready. His hope and his determination had never gone.

He had run far and seen many things since he had started out. An old man can not remember all that he has seen and done. What he can remember, he remembers with greater clarity and often with greater pleasure than he does when he is young and remembers more. As he ran along the road, the old gingerbread man remembered with pleasure the mowers. There had been five of them. They were not such men as the threshers who had run with scorn and spite in their hearts. The mowers were men of good will. They strove to beat him, but they felt no malice when they were beaten. They were his brothers, and he had to outrun them. That was the way of the world. Why must brothers vie one with another so that there is but one winner? He had no understanding of such things. He knew only that the mowers had run well, that they were his brothers and that he had beaten them. It was pleasant to remember the mowers as he ran along the road.

He liked to think of other things as he ran. He liked to think of the great Fig Newton. The exploits of Newton he had always followed with great interest. The whole world knew of Newton; he was often written of in the papers and spoken of on the radio. He would have enjoyed meeting the famous Fig. They might have run together. He would not have vied with Fig Newton. They would have

FAIRY TALES FOR ADULTS

run and talked, but there would have been no talk of a winner. He could have learned much about endurance from the great Newton. And perhaps he could have told him how to break away, clean and fast, from an oven. But you speak foolishness, he said to himself. Newton has no need of your instruction! You are becoming childish, old man. Keep your mind on matters at hand.

"How do you feel, legs?" he said aloud.

His legs remained silent. That was a good thing. When they replied they always spoke of something that was not agreeable to hear. They spoke of cramps and of pain.

The road curved to the left now and ran parallel to a canal. Tall sedges grew on the bank of the canal and they bent and swayed as the air swept through them. They were graceful and elegant as a woman is graceful and elegant, and the sight of them stirred in the old man memories of the cow.

She was a brown and white cow and she had run with the old man. How sleek and silken her hair was. She was a beautiful cow and the old man had loved her. She ran well. They ran because there was joy in the running. "She was my sister," he said aloud. "She was my sister and I loved her." But in truth, he thought, I loved her not as a brother loves a sister. She was lovely and I desired her. But I outran her. I loved her and I respected her and I outran her.

That was the way of the world. There is joy in running and there is joy in winning and the old man was a winner. There was loneliness in the winning, but that was the way of the world.

He could feel the evening coming. Though there were no clouds in the sky and the sun had not yet set, he could feel in the air the first intimation of the chill that the night would bring. The road ahead of him dipped and then it rose again and then it turned to the right and led him into a grove of trees. The leaves of these trees trembled as a gentle wind touched and moved them, and they filtered the sunlight so that a hundred dancing shafts of light dappled the way before him. How lovely the trees are, he thought. You might stop running and sit beneath a tree. How pleasant it must be to see the trees, not as one sees them as they go swiftly past, but as a painter sees them, still and serene. How pleasant it must be to rest.

"You are a fool, old man," he said aloud. "You are a runner and runners do not rest."

Still, it would be good to rest. It would be good not to run.

"What is the use of such thought?" he asked himself. "There is no use in such thought. Such thoughts are treacherous. I must keep my mind on matters at hand. I am a runner. I must run and I must not think foolish thoughts."

The further he ran into the trees the darker it became. It was not the darkness of night but the darkness of a forest. It was not a grove of trees into which he had run but a forest and it was dark in the forest.

I hope that this forest is not a large one, he thought. Night is coming and that will bring darkness enough.

In the deepening shadows the road became indistinct and oddly luminescent. It had a pale, livid shine like that on the belly of a dead trout. The road made sudden, unpredictable turns as it wound through the trees, and the old man was forced to look down upon his feet. A good runner will as a matter of choice never look at his feet. He looks at the road ahead. He focuses on an ever-receding spot ten or eleven feet ahead of him. But the road was uneven now, pitted with dangerous holes and overgrown with vines. The old man grew cautious. Better to run slow than risk injury, he thought.

Time passed. Perhaps an hour. The trees began to thin and the air grew lighter. It was not so light as when he went into the forest. It was twilight. But there was now more light that there had been. There was sufficient light to permit the old man to resume his accustomed pace. As the road became more visible, it also became wider and straighter and less perilous. There was never a time when the old man was without caution, but conditions now permitted him to relax his vigilance. He had been as a fist, clenched and tight. He was now at ease again—watchful and alert and at ease.

On his right he could see a hayfield. The hay had been mown and it was stacked in high golden mounds. The breeze that came from across the field carried a faint, sweet odor, and the old man remembered the horse. "Horse," he said aloud, "you were my best competitor—the most beautiful, the most noble."

FAIRY TALES FOR ADULTS

He had been younger then. He had beaten the threshers and the mowers. He had gone far beyond them. He had beaten others. He did not remember all of the others. He had beaten the cow. In his heart he remembered, always, the cow. But the horse was his most noble, most memorable competitor.

"How swiftly, how beautifully you ran," he said aloud. "I loved you and I respected you and I beat you."

The horse was gray. He had a white spot on his nose. His legs were well-muscled and strong, and he had powerful lungs. Such powerful lungs the old man had never before encountered. The horse ran without tiring. He ran as though the joy of running sustained and encouraged him. They ran, the two of them, shoulder to shoulder. For hours they ran so, neither ahead of the other. That had not happened to the old man before. He was surprised but he was not alarmed. He did not doubt that he could outrun the horse.

All day they had run and all night. It was dawn before the horse began to show the first signs of exhaustion. He began to pant and, at last, to lag behind the old man. Then, suddenly, the horse stopped running and fell to his knees. How quickly it had happened! How sad the old man had felt. And now, remembering the beautiful, noble horse, the old man said aloud, "I am sorry, horse. You were my brother. I loved you and I beat you."

It was evening now and a full moon had risen. The old man turned onto a wide pathway which rose over a series of grassy hills before descending into a long flat valley. He was running well. The night air was keen but, warmed by his running, he did not feel the chill.

I hope that I do not tire, he thought. I do not have that strength that I had when I began to run. My legs are old legs.

"Do not be a fool," he said aloud. "If you have less of a young man's strength, do you not have more of an old man's experience? If your legs feel pain and your lungs grow tired, have you not learned to suffer and endure? I will not think of old age and of pain. I will think of Fig Newton."

Then he saw him. The path on which the old man was running crossed a meadow, then, veering to the right, it followed a rustic wooden fence. It was by this fence, under a large maple tree, that he lay in wait. The old man did not at first see his body. It was his eyes he saw—staring, evil eyes gleaming in the darkness like coals. A fox.

And then he was beside him. It seemed to the old man that it had taken no time for the fox to move from the tree to his side, so swiftly and so abruptly had the crafty creature come upon him. In the bright moonlight the old man saw the sharp white teeth in the slavering mouth of the beast, and he knew at once that it was no competitor who ran by his side, but a dangerous foe who meant to kill him.

So, fox, you intend to eat me, he thought. But I am not an old gingerbread man who intends to be eaten. First you must catch me.

The old man pulled ahead of the fox and for miles the two ran together, the old man always a few feet ahead of the fox.

You are swift, fox, the old man thought. You are swift and you run well, but you did not know that I am the winner and undisputed champion. Now you will learn.

All night they ran. The bitter coppery taste came into the old man's mouth and the small sharp knife pricked his lungs.

I have tasted and felt these before, the old man thought. They are matters of little importance. I will think only about the road ahead. I will keep my lead. I will keep my head free from doubt.

When the sun rose, the two runners were still in the long flat valley. The road upon which they ran seemed to follow, always at such a distance that it could not be seen, a river. But though it was out of sight, the river could be heard. The old man heard, or thought he heard, the sound of rushing water. He was glad of the sound. The water, he thought, runs well.

The sun had risen above the line of tree to the east and the old man could see his shadow. And always, only a few feet to his rear, he felt the presence of the fox. Only occasionally did he turn to look at the fox—to catch a glimpse of its red, lean body and its panting, vicious mouth. He did not need to see the fox. He knew always that it was there behind him.

It was still quite early in the morning when he legs began to speak. They spoke of cramping and pain.

FAIRY TALES FOR ADULTS

"Be quite, legs!" he said aloud. "The fox had four legs that grow tired and weak. You are but two. I have the advantage."

He ignored the cramping and the pain and ran on.

They ran for hours, the fox never gaining upon the old man. The old man was tired as he had never before been tired. He felt pain such as he had never before felt. I must endure, he thought, as I endured when I ran against my brother the horse.

But you were young then. Since you ran against the beautiful, noble horse you have grown old.

He drove this doubt from his mind. Such ideas are poison, he thought. I must rid myself of them as I would spit out filth.

It was noon or close to noon when the old man realized that all was lost. The road which for miles had followed the river turned at an abrupt right angle and led downward through a gulch with high steep banks into the river. There was no bridge across the river. There was no ferry. Those who took this road and wished to cross the river to the opposite side must swim. There was no other way.

Water was as fatal to the gingerbread man as coffee is to a donut. He could be in water only briefly before he began to dissolve.

After an instance's deliberation, the old man turned to his left and began to run along the bank of the river, parallel to its flow. But the coarse sharp gravel on the bank slowed his pace and soon the fox was at his heels.

You have beaten me fox, the old man thought. You have beaten me and you wish to eat me. It is time to die. So be it. I have lived my life. I have run well. But you will not eat me fox. I know a way to beat you yet.

And the old man jumped into the river. He could not swim, but he ran as fast as he could until the water was up to his chin. But the fox, who was an excellent swimmer, was instantly after him, and before the old man dissolved, the fox had him in his jaws. He pulled the old man to the bank and ate him.

The fox let the head of the gingerbread man drop from his jaws, and in his haste and in his greed he did not notice the head lying on the bank by the river. In the evening it was discovered by two magpies.

"What is this?" the female asked.

"It is the corpse of a brown beetle," the male replied. And with this, he tasted a bit of the head to test it fitness as food. "It has a strange, foreign flavor," he said. "It must have come from another country. It is hard and tough, but it will nourish us. Eat."

And together they ate the last of the old gingerbread man.

Beauty Abeyant: a Comedy

T. S. Eliot

Characters:
Lord Egbert Leroy
Lady Millicent Leroy, *his wife*
Barrett and Bertrand, *his bachelor sons*
Belle, *his daughter, eighteen years old*
Mysterious Stranger
Teddy Prince, *an American movie star*
Dora, *parlor maid*
Evil Godmother
Chorus, *seven Fairy Godmothers*

Scene: *The drawing room of Dormant, the family estate of Lord Leroy: a large room richly and comfortably furnished. Seated at the rear of the room are seven Fairy Godmothers located in a large bay window. In their midst—in a commanding, elevated position—sits the Evil Godmother. When the members of the chorus speak, they stand; otherwise they remain seated, intently observing the action.*

Time: *Early spring*

145

David R. Ewbank

Chorus

Gracious blessings, bountifully bestowed
Upon this house and hearth—blighted,
Brought to naught, never perfected,
Lying neglected, negated by lying.
The blooms do not flourish nor the buds fructify,
Nor can the song of the skylark be heard
In the stifled air of the withered wood—
Only the croak of a frog, the crepitation of crickets,
The dry cough of a closing door,
A clattering shutter, occluding light.

Evil Godmother

None may exclude the inexcludable,
The bane in the balm, the ill in the idyll,
The flaw in the pattern, the fly in the ointment,
The mendacity that misdirects
The purposing maker's poised hand,
The vanity that vitiates
The incipient promise of the inchoate vision.
Now, ensconced in my rightful station
Among these seven—see! Their nature's
Chastened. My sway is now secure.
By spindle, by cunning, I've cast the spell
That works to perfect my purpose fell.

Chorus

The weaver imagines he fashions the web,
But Time, the warp, and Fate, the woof,
Weave a vaguer, vaster pattern
And the vain weaver himself is woven.
Do not suppose a purpose accomplished,
A plan perfected or a pattern finished,
Until the plenitude of Time
Brings into view the ambiguous result
Of firm projects, ineffectively executed,

FAIRY TALES FOR ADULTS

Of casual velleities, successfully effectuated.
For now this estate slumbers, stagnates.
An ancient lineage, an ancient name,
Enduring for centuries, comes to an end.
The male heirs, unmarried, childless.
For now the inhabitants of this house sleep—
But the spider's at work in the upstairs window,
And the mole burrows under the beech tree.
We must wait and watch—wait and watch.

[*Enter* Lord Egbert, *carrying a potted plant, and*
Lady Millicent Leroy.]
Lord Egbert

This Kafir-lily's looking frail.
It doesn't matter what I do:
Water it, it withers; don't
Water it, it shrinks and wilts.
I thought perhaps that placing it here
Would buck it up; the sun's much brighter
Here in this room, and I hope . . . .

Lacy Millicent
Really,
Eggy, why you even bother
To concern yourself with horticulture
I'll never know. You should know by now
You have absolutely no aptitude.
You're always disappointed, dear.

Lord Egbert
But horticulture's my hobby, Millie.
[*He places the plant on a sideboard.*]

Lady Millicent
It's strange you should find satisfaction in just
That pastime for which you're perfectly unfitted.

147

David R. Ewbank

Still, your hobby—if hopeless—is harmless,
So grub away! But gracious, look!
It's nearly time for cocktails. Now,
You go get dressed, and don't dawdle.

          [*Exit* Lord Egbert]
Oh dear! What was it I meant to do?
Oh yes, I must see if there's sherry. Perhaps
Our guest prefers sherry. I seem to recall
That he does. Or was it whiskey? Oh dear!
It was such a long while ago. Where
Does the time go?

          Chorus
      Down the drain!
It seeps—cunning, unrecallable.
Clocks measure but cannot mark
The promise and the peril of Time.
Fate inhabits every fleeting
Moment. A single second's breadth
Is space enough to shape a life.
One can't undo a deed once done,
Nor amend the needful deed undone.
There's no escape from the self-laid snare
Of choices made, of chances missed.

          Lady Millicent
The question was rhetorical! It's quite
Unnecessary to say sooth
Apropos of every passing remark.
Decorum, ladies! Keep your comments
To yourselves, please. I'm expecting a guest
A very astute, discerning guest.
He is fully attuned to the finer dimensions
And as such will sense your presence here—
May even, I think, see you there,

FAIRY TALES FOR ADULTS

But he won't be in need of your timely exhortations.
And besides, you know that no one in the family,
My self excepted, sees or hears you.

Chorus

Could the benighted behold, the knot would unravel.
Could the heedless harken, the clot would dissolve.
But always the acid etches the plate,
And Doom, indelible, is inscribed on the slate.

Lady Millicent

Yes, yes! Quite so! Now pray—silence!
I've ever so much on my mind to contend with.

[*Enter* Barrett, Bertrand *and* Belle]

[*Belle, a stunningly beautiful girl, sits on a sofa and throughout the following action says nothing. She takes little interest in what is being said or done. She lounges on a sofa, leafs through a magazine, yawns, looks bored, and finally falls asleep.*]

Oh there you are, children. How chic you're looking.
Belle, you're delightful, as always, dear.
Sit down and rest. Our guest will arrive
Any minute now. I must just check
On something. But what? I forget.

Chorus
Sherry.

Lady Millicent

Ah yes. Thank you. Now Bertie and Barry,
Try not to quarrel. I'll be right back.
I must chat with Dora about the hors oeuvres.

DAVID R. EWBANK

[*Exit* Lady Millicent]
[*Barrett and Bertrand sit. Bertrand hums a simple, repetitive ditty.*]

Barrett

Mama seems to be in her usual muddle.
Who *is* this bloke she's invited, Bertie?
She mentioned a name—D. X. Mackinaw, was it?
I've forgotten. Some government fellow, I think—
Some puffed-up pooh-bah from some sort of ministry.
Culture, perhaps. Or Home Affairs.

Bertrand

Maybe the man's an old flame of Mama's.
He could have conducted affairs closer
To home than we think.

Barrett

Heavens forfend!
What a rum thought. One always thinks
Of one's mother as . . . well—pure and passionless!

Bertrand

She can't have been. *We're* here, aren't we?
She must have fancied father—once.

Barrett

Facts are facts. Still, one thinks of father as . . .
Bertie—it doesn't bear thinking about!
[*They sit opposite each other and Bertrand again begins to hum the same ditty.*]
I wish you'd stop humming that horrid tune;
It's really becoming a beastly bore!
Is that song what you've been swotting away at
All this time, upstairs in your studio?

FAIRY TALES FOR ADULTS

Bertrand

Don't be waspish. You know quite well
I've devoted my self these seven years
To my grand opus, a five-act opera,
Queene of the Faeries, a serial treatment
Of two or three of Spenser's tales,
Reimagined for a modern audience,
Set in a space station, orbiting the earth,
And performed by an all-male cast of forty.
This silly little tune's a mere trifle.
Who knows why such nonsense pops into one's head?

Barrett

May I expect, within my lifetime,
To hear your magnum opus?

Bertrand

Oh,

Euterpe takes her time, you know;
She can be a bloody, balky flirt.
For months now I've been baffled by
A tangle in my twelve-tone row.

Barrett

"O O O how time flies by,
Before you can blink,
You're old and you think,
When did I kiss my youth good-by?"

Bertrand

Stop it, Barry! You're quite absurd.
These jejune jingles you favor us with—
And you have the face to fault my tunes!
Is that insipid doggerel a fair sample
Of the classic poem you've been chipping away at
These many years?

151

David R. Ewbank

Barrett
Down, mastiff!
I hope my *Hadrianiad*—
My twelve canto epic tale
Of the tragic love of the enamored emperor
For the lovely lad Antinoüs—
May anon be complete. Just now I'm a bit
Blocked by a hitch in the tricky hexameters.
And as for my jingles, it's just as you say:
Why knows why such nonsense pops into one's head?

Chorus
Crossed threads! Contrary theses!
Who knows the word, who kens the way
To straighten, in time, such tangled contention?
The past and the future meet and mingle
In every perilous present moment.
And always the falcon flies at dawn;
At dusk the furrowing plow is dropped.

[*Enter* Lord Egbert, Lady Millicent *and* Mysterious Stranger]
Lady Millicent
Children, see who's just now come!
Let me introduce my dear old friend:
Denholm—Barrett and Bertrand.
[*They stand to receive the guest.*]

Mysterious Stranger
[*He shakes their hands.*]
Delighted.

Lady Millicent
And my beautiful daughter, Belle.

Fairy Tales for Adults

Mysterious Stranger
Delighted.
[*Belle, not yet quite asleep, acknowledges her guest's presence with a nod
of her head.*]

Lady Millicent
What may we offer you? Sherry? Whiskey?

Mysterious Stranger
I've ventured to bring my own vintage—
A potent potation, I warn you, one
That produces unexpected effects.
[*He removes a large bottle from his briefcase.*]

Lady Millicent
How very intriguing! Eggy, dear,
Please serve us, won't you?
[*As the conversation proceeds, Lord Egbert opens the bottle, fills glasses
and serves the drink to everyone but Belle, who is now asleep.*]
Well, shall we sit?
[*They sit*]

Barrett
You come to us from the city, sir.
I understand you've something to do
With government. Have I got that right?
What's your special bailiwick?

Mysterious Stranger
The Ministry of Truth.

Barrett
I must
Confess—this is the first I've heard
Of such a post.

153

DAVID R. EWBANK

Mysterious Stranger
I'm not surprised.

Barrett
[*jocularly*]
And does the position impose on you
The task of always telling the truth?

Mysterious Stranger
[*seriously*]
Certainly.
[*An awkward silence ensues*]

Bertrand
[*diplomatically*]
Well, I'm sure that I
Should never succeed at such a task.

Mysterious Stranger

[*rudely*]
I share your conviction, sir.

Bertrand
I say!

Lady Millicent
Here are our drinks. Thank you, my dear.
To what shall we toast? Denholm—a toast.

Chorus
One rock may launch an avalanche,
A single drop may breach the dam.
A word—intended, meant to tell—
No less a casual, careless word
May serve to heal or harm—may kill.

FAIRY TALES FOR ADULTS

Be wary! Every passing pulse
Of time is potent. Now—the tick
That flickers, quick, twixt soon and gone!
Every now shapes destinies.

Evil Godmother
What is this stifling, foul miasma
Rising like a lethal mist!

Mysterious Stranger
To truth!

Barrett
Just so!

Bertrand
Here, here!

Lord Egbert
Jolly good!
[*They drink. A sudden transformation alters the features and demeanor of Barrett and Bertrand.*]

Barrett
My word!

Bertrand
What's this!

Mysterious Stranger
The truth! The truth
Shall set this household free. Hear!
Barrett—eldest, first-born scion:
You are not a Homer, nor even a Houseman.
Curb your pretension. Face facts.
Bertrand—scion second-born:

155

DAVID R. EWBANK

You are not a Bach, not even an Offenbach.
Abate your ambition. Expel ego.

Barrett

It's strange, but somehow, as you were speaking,
In a sudden, visionary stroke,
I recognized the rectitude
Of your assessment, harsh but honest.

Bertrand

Barry, beloved brother! I
Too had a vision. That tune in my head—
It perfectly fits that jingle of yours.
[*He sings.*]
"O O O how times flies by,
Before you can blink,
You're old and you think
When did I kiss my youth good-by?"

Barrett

Bertie, it's true! Why we two might become
A famous duo: Leroy and Leroy—
Master composers of music hall songs!
[*They rise and embrace each other.*]

Mysterious Stranger

Go in peace and seek your salvation!
The road you will travel is not the road
Of saints and sages. Yet your way
Avoids the darksome Vale of Deception,
Skirts the Swamp of Self-Delusion
And the Dismal Bog of Mendacity.
Go, resigned to your mediocrity!
Your lowly lot has its compensations:
The ephemeral plaudits of the fickle mob
And sundry showy prizes—brass

Plaques and silver statuettes.

                    Barrett
Good! Bertie, let us go at once.
Our brave collaboration starts
Today!

                    Bertrand
        Corking! Lead the way.
[*Exit* Barrett *and* Bertrand, *arm in arm*]

                Evil Godmother
I faint! I languish! Air! Air!

            Mysterious Stranger
And now, Millicent, if I may, I suggest
That the time has come for *you* to tell
The truth.

                Lady Millicent
        Indeed. Egbert, dear,
If what I say's abrupt and brusque,
Forgive me. But, forgive me more
For being slow: for keeping secret
All these years a circumstance
That you've a right to know. Remember:
What I did I did because
I thought that it was best—best
For you as well as me. Well—
That dreadful time during the war—
You were home on furlough, before being shipped
To France. And then—those terrible months,
Living in trenches—a death-in-life!
I told you then to expect a third
Child when you returned, and you
Wrote back to say that the blessed news

Soothed like a cooling dram in hell.
And then—much later, you returned
And took such deep delight in Belle.
I simply could not bring myself
To tell the truth. But Denholm here
Insists the time has come and I'm
In full agreement. Eggy. You
Are not Belle's father!

Lord Egbert

[*astounded*]
Not!

Lady Millicent
No!

Lord Egbert
Then who?

Mysterious Stranger
I!

Lord Egbert
You!

Mysterious Stranger
Yes!

Lord Egbert
You rogue!

Mysterious Stranger
Moderate your rage!
The time's propitious for a counter confession
From you. All those months when Millicent
Thought you were missing in action—you were

FAIRY TALES FOR ADULTS

In fact a prisoner of war, finally
Freed, but confined for a time to a clinic
In Caen, being treated for a chronic illness
Contracted in the prison camp.
A certain amorous episode
With a pretty nurse transpired, did
It not? A pretty American nurse?
It's time for you to tell your wife.

Lord Egbert

What nerve, sir! How can you know
About deeds, dared and done
Long ago, and long ago
Regretted, and mercifully forgotten?

Mysterious Stranger

The Ministry of Truth has many
Means we may rely upon
To aid us. I'm afraid that you
Deceive yourself to think you can
Dismiss your sins, immure them in
A safe, settled, receding past.
The past is always with us. With us
Literally—as soon you'll see.
I advise you to speak, and don't prevaricate.

Lord Egbert

It happened, Millie, as he says.
I was young. I am sorry. I betrayed your trust.
Once! Only once. But since
She went her way and I went mine,
And since I've never heard from her
Again, what gain is there—what
Useful purpose can now be served
By bringing back those distant days?

DAVID R. EWBANK

Mysterious Stranger
Allow me to produce the purpose, sir.
There's one waiting in the library.
[*Exit* Mysterious Stranger]

Lord Egbert
What
Can that meddling fellow mean?

Chorus
The past is intractable—is ineluctable.
A lever depressed, a spring released—
Machinery is set in motion.
Slow though the cogs may turn,
Consequences, soon or late,
Are sure. The truth—the quickening truth
Will out.

Evil Godmother
Aiyeee! Aiyeee! I suffer!

Lord Egbert
It appears, Millie, that we must both
Forgive each other's sins. Agreed?

Lady Millicent
Quite, my dear! I freely acquit you—
Both for the deed, and for the deceit.

Lord Egbert
And I, you—heartily and happily.
[*They embrace each other.*]

FAIRY TALES FOR ADULTS

[*Enter* Mysterious Stranger *and* Teddy Prince]
Mysterious Stranger
I'm pleased to present Mister Teddy Prince,
The famous American movie star.
He's over here from Hollywood
Filming . . . forgive me, I've forgotten.

Teddy Prince
The Labyrinth of Love.

Mysterious Stranger
Ah yes—
The Labyrinth of Love. "Prince"
Is not your natal name, I think.

Teddy Prince
Oh no, my real last name is "Smith."
My agent said that that name stinks.
For films you need a fancy name.

Mysterious Stranger
But "Smith" is not your father's name?

Teddy Prince
I never knew my father's name.
Till recently I never knew
My father—until you got in touch
With me I thought that he was dead.
But then I learned that Lord Leroy
Had met my mother and . . .

Lord Egbert
Good God!
Was "Margaret" your mother's name?

DAVID R. EWBANK

Teddy Prince
Yes sir.

Lord Egbert
Son!

Teddy Prince
Dad!

Evil Godmother
Damn!
[*LordEgbert and Teddy Prince embrace each other. The Evil Godmother falls lifeless to the floor. The seven Fairy Godmothers open a window and throw her body outside.*]

Lord Egbert
Ted, my boy, tell me—your mother . . .
Is she well?

Teddy Prince
She died when I was only
Eight. I was raised by a maiden aunt.

Lord Egbert
Well now that the truth is known, would
You like to take, at last, your legal,
Rightful name—"Leroy"?

Teddy Prince
I'd
Be honored, sir. Of course, I'd still
Be "Teddy Prince" in public. That's
A standard clause in my contract with Glitter
Productions.

FAIRY TALES FOR ADULTS

Lord Egbert
Of course, one can't change that.

Teddy Prince
It seems funny—having, finally,
A father. I feel I hardly know you.

Lord Egbert
It *is* strange. We must become
Better acquainted.

Mysterious Stranger
Indeed! But best
Remember: Time, inexorable Time,
Ushers in the transient seasons,
Compels the ceaseless, unflagging flux
Of generation—of disintegration.
Seasons change. People change.
It is wise to deem that every day
The face of a spouse—a father—a son
Is the countenance of a stranger, quite
Capable of fresh surprises.

Lord Egbert
[*curtly*]
Thank you, I'm sure.

Teddy Prince
Whatever you say.
But there's someone here I haven't met.
Who *is* that girl, asleep on the sofa—
My sister?

Lady Millicent
Dear boy, how rude we've been!
It's all rather complicated.

Perhaps it's best to put it this way:
Belle, there, is your step-sister;
Your father is not her father.

Teddy Prince

Wow, is she ever a luscious peach!
Ernst Reissnagel—he's my director—
Is looking for a girl who looks
Like her—a blooming, natural blonde—
To play the part of Ariadne.
Belle would be the perfect choice.
Can she sing? The movie's a musical
In Technicolor with a cast of thousands.

Lady Millicent

Why, actually, Belle has a beautiful voice.
[*Teddy walks to the sofa, bends down and kisses Belle on the cheek. Belle
awakens, sees Teddy, and beams with delight.*]

Belle

Teddy Prince! Thank Providence!
You've finally come! I've waited for you
All my life. My love, I've seen
Every one of your marvelous films;
The Man I Married is my favorite.

Teddy Prince

Belle, would you be my leading lady
In the movie we're making now?

Belle

[*rapturously*]
Oh yes!
[*They embrace each other.*]

FAIRY TALES FOR ADULTS

Teddy Prince
Have you got a phone? I've got to get
In touch with Ernst. I want to tell him
I've finally found our Ariadne.

Lady Millicent
The telephone's in the hallway

Teddy Prince
Thanks!
Come with me, Belle. Boy, this is swell!
[*Exit* Belle *and* Teddy Prince, *hand in hand*]

Mysterious Stranger
I think we may safely speculate
That those two beautiful children will wed—
That the name "Leroy" will not expire.

Lady Millicent
Oh Eggy! This is the very thing
I'd hoped would happen. You've yearned in vain
For years for a young male heir. Our sons
Have proved to be, in this respect . . .
How shall I say . . . disappointing?

Lord Egbert
Disinclined.

Mysterious Stranger
And so, you see,
Lord Egbert, all has turned out well.
The enmity you feel toward me,
However understandable,
May weaken when you come to see
That the consequence of my offense—
Of *our* offense—though unintended—in

165

The end—proved to be a blessing.

Lady Millicent
Oh Eggy, Denholm's right! Doesn't
Fate unfold in wondrous ways!

Lord Egbert
As I forgave my wife, so I
Freely grant you forgiveness, sir!
[*Lord Egbert and the Mysterious Stranger embrace each other.*]

Chorus
[*The Fairy Godmothers don party hats and celebrate by tooting horns, shaking noisemakers, and throwing confetti at one another.*]
Dawn! Daybreak!
This house is awake!
Our blessings—once blighted
By arrogance—benighted
By falsehood—insidious
By guile—invidious
May now be enjoyed
Unimpaired, unalloyed.
Our object is won,
Our work here is done.
[*Exit* Chorus *through the open window.*]

Lord Egbert
Why look, Millie, my Kafir lily's
Blooming!

Lady Millicent
Why so it is! Success
At last, my dear!
[*Enter* Dora *with a tray of hors o'euvres.*]

FAIRY TALES FOR ADULTS

Dora
M'laidy, 'ere's
That tray of tiny tit-bits ... Aaoooow!

Lady Millicent
Why Dora, dear, what *is* the matter?

Mysterious Stranger
I suspect that Dora sees something—
Or rather, doesn't see—something
That she expected to see. Am I right?

Dora
It's them spooks that's us'ally sittin' there
In the winder. They're gone! They al'ays give me
Such a fright. Can't say I'll miss 'em.

Lady Millicent
Why Dora, I had no idea.

Dora
I thought the 'ouse was 'aunted.

Mysterious Stranger
So
It was! Now a new day dawns!

Lord Egbert
I can't imagine what you mean—
But let it go. I've learned to live
With mysteries. And you, Millie,
The most mysterious of all.
You're very deep.

DAVID R. EWBANK

Lady Millicent
No matter, dear.
And now—the cocktails. This happy conclusion
To a tangled tale warrants a toast.
Now Denholm, it's been so long—I don't
Recall. Tell me your drink of choice
Again. Sherry? Whiskey?

Mysterious Stranger
Gin.

[*They laugh.*]

[*Curtain*]

The Glass Slipper:
Confession of a Happy
Wedded Prince

Vladimir Nabokov

Cendrillon. A sudden sibilance mildly subsiding to a rich Gallic resonance. The name, like the radiant blaze the bewitching nymph ignites, an astonished exclamation and a lingering wonder! Sound aptly aping sensation. Cenerentola. An aria *in breve*! Cenicienta. Sweetest, most adorable *senorita*! Euphonious euphorient! Then, alas, a sad declension to Cinderella, the miserable moniker by which my peerless American princess was in gloomy reality nominated. Only one slippery step removed from Aschenputtle—that Teutonic mud puddle, that guttural gutter! But I will have none of it. I refuse to submit to the tyrannous fiat of Fact. In that most tuneful language which ever welled and rippled from the nimble tongue of man—in, that is to say, my native Bonovak (accent on the last of the three syllables, silent *k*, the ultimate vowel long and luscious—an enchanting vocalic rather resembling the susurration of a Bonovian dove) her name is Allito. Allito I call her. As Allito I claim her.

How long, how passionately I awaited her coming! Kind Papa waxed fretful. Dearest Mama wept bitter tears. When, oh when would I meet and mate with the maid who would mother the royal heir? Dames and duchesses came and went. Aristocratic aspirants of every rank and stripe turned up. Thumbs down. Ruthless Time swept the accumulating seconds into the dustbin of the past, but no marriage contract was signed, no union consummated. Was I impotent? Inverted? Physicians prodded my soma. Shrinks probed my psyche. A Freudian shaman with his bag of complexes and cathexes performed his farcical hocus-pocus by scrutinizing my dreams and sabotaging my associations. (River. Mouth. Ach zo! Oral fixation!) A Jungian charlatan with his portmanteau of archedalas and mantypes dived into my collective unconscious. I took pity on a kindly, bumbling, sweet-tempered Adlerian and played along with his game. He was inordinately grateful, poor thing: he was *so* inclined to feel inferior. I was judged to be physically capable of successful child siring, and mentally .... Ah well, shall we just say that I was no more strung-out or mixed-up than the next functioning neurotic.

Why, then, no spouse—no spawn? What was the key to the conundrum?

I took scrupulous care to withhold my secret from all those prying crackpots and pompous nincompoops who would have fouled my beautiful passion with some beastly, sordid label. "Foot fetishist" they would have pronounced. Frightful phrase! Shades of gibbering aborigines genuflecting to a blood-spattered juju! No—no psychogenic distemper, no snazzy, new-fangled syndrome cooked up by some cockeyed alienist caused the long delay which was (since the hand that writes these words will be inert clay long before my confession reaches the eyes of any living reader, I may—pre-posthumously, as it were—reveal the truth) epiphanic, not paraphiliac in origin.

I had, you see, a vision. Oh, nothing in the ectoplasm line. Nothing paranormal or hallucinatory. My vision was palpably, blessedly material. She was not a fellow citizen of Bonovia. Indeed, she had never seen the pristine snow-capped peaks of my native land. Had not sipped that heady, exhilarating elixir—Bonovian air, nor savored the nacreous nuances of the pale light which gleams, tenuous and tender, upon the rocks and trees and fields of my superb

FAIRY TALES FOR ADULTS

sub-Arctic kingdom. She was conceived, nursed and nurtured in southern climes, my primal, reproachless Eve, and it was on a golden beach, under sunny skies, swept by mild favonian zephyrs, (we were, for the benefit of the bluntly literal, in Greece) that I first encountered my future—my fate. Her name was . . . . but what does it matter? It was a commonplace, humble name, no less unfitting than the absurd appellation of her avatar, Cinderella. I shall persist in calling her Eve. She dwelt in a rented villa which neighbored our own, a resplendent residence far more opulent and ostentatious than our comfy but unpretentious royal retreat. Her father was a shipbuilding magnate, bald top-side but luxuriantly, repulsively hirsute below. Her mother, a retired but by no means retiring cinema starlet who spent her abundant leisure darkening her epidermis so as to achieve an oddly unnatural sorrel effect which she inaccurately referred to as her "tan." (*Vex spermátia abasáta blosse trebæsse vaxēt*—to quote from our incomparable Bonovian saga *Kăi Kălavŏ*. "From what lowly germs lovely flowers grow!") She was fourteen, my senior by one year. In furtive moments, stolen from the benignly inadequate vigilance of supervising adults—in sea-carved grottoes and behind sheltering dunes my precocious preceptress initiated me into those secular sacraments which may or may not, as the old adage has it, make the world go round, but which indubitably set my young wits reeling.

She was beautiful, brunette, slim, pneumatic and passionate. But these traits, admirable without doubt, are shared by hordes of comely, well-fashioned lasses. My sea sprite was unique. She had feet! Such feet as come to adorn and delight the world only rarely in an entire generation's lavish output of work-a-day, usable, commonplace, down-to-earth extremities! Ah, Mnemosyne—Mother of all Arts, beneficent Curator and provident Preserver, I bow to thee in gratitude for the eidetic image treasured in the museum of my mind, the *chef d'oeuvre* of a supreme master, the most prized of memories which yet inflames my spirit and fires my loins. Her right foot, to begin with that member which I sighted first, was a perfect petite poem. It was encased in a clumsy sabot of some sort—a heavy, unsightly affair designed, I suppose, to assist locomotion across

171

tracts of speed-impeding sand. With a single careless gesture she kicked the encumbrance aside. That swift, insouciant exposure was an imperious, life-altering, thaumaturgic moment—a divine divulgation—a numinous theophany! I was as ogling Actæon, mute and astonished, though in my case it was not from my head that a horny appendage sprouted. Lenient reader, permit a doting miser a brief inventory of his riches. The ankle, slim and svelte. An eloquent joint, so to speak—articulate beyond the norm. How fervently I longed to kiss it, and how frequently I appeased my longing. The arch. What a monstrous maladaptation, what a sad desecration that whenever the human animal assumes its famed erect position so sublime a feature is necessarily pressed against dull, dumb earth and is thus hidden from inspection and lost to admiration. Could you only have learned to walk on your hands, my darling Eve, your feet proudly aloft in the air, magnificently naked! And the toes, that charming line-up of adorable look-alikes: big sister toe—Margaret, statuesque second toe—Isabel, clever third toe—Theresa, shy fourth toe—Violet, and droll little baby toe—Pansy. What happy hours I spent playing "Happy Family" and "Tom Thumb Went a'Courting" and "Bad Doctor Digit" with those lovable, lickable sisters!

Now the left foot. Ditto. Ten toes. Double bliss!

See us as profile figures on a Grecian urn. She: seated, regal in her commanding beauty. Me: kneeling, supplicant, ithyphallic—kissing her extended foot. An antique snapshot. Are we not a smart, eye-catching pair—our impetuous ardor fast frozen for eternity?

I have said that Eve (orient gem; precious playmate) was my future—an avowal perhaps misleading, though not, if understood aright, untrue. I did not (as slangy Allito would put it) "keep up" with Eve—did not woo and wed my incomparably desirable nixie. (But here again, trusting reader, I am perhaps, by invoking Allito, leading you up a garden path. Let me assure you that my beloved wife does not know, does not even suspect, that there was an Edenic episode in my past—that she is the faultless copy of an exquisite original. Heaven forfend! My Allito is a jealous minx. I employ her terminology without her knowledge or consent. And so—to quote her once again—please "keep this under your hat.") At the end of

FAIRY TALES FOR ADULTS

that wonderful idyll, the thirteenth summer of my life, the world with its dreary rules and rituals interposed and with a brutal hand separated Eve from her Adam. I was never to see her again. I followed her career in gossip columns—watched her grow in rotogravure. (An aristocratic British suitor. A splashy wedding in Athens. A lover. A scandal. A divorce. A new alliance with some rich, beefy, mustached playboy.) I caught a final glimpse of her in a sordid London tabloid, overweight and slightly tipsy, shouldn't wonder—toasting some duke or other with an upraised glass of champagne. This just weeks before her fatal accident in a speedboat off Corfu.

In that world of reported rumors and captured shadows Eve transmogrified into an everyday, unexceptional matron—ample of waist and thick of ankle. But those vulgar public images in no way altered and never replaced the invincible vision which I preserve safe and changeless in my mind and which I may at will recall. And though I was fated never to see the mutable, material Eve again, she was in sooth my future, i.e. the indelible memory of her unexampled foot haunted all my coming days and determined the course of my life.

That pompous pederast Socrates tries to persuade us that Forms are Ideal in the sense that they exist only in our minds—that "appearances" in the world of space and time are but inferior copies of immaterial concepts which alone are real. Silly old Socrates! Had he ever seen Eve's feet he would have changed his tune. Those glorious appendages were ideal in the sense that they were perfect, and you may invest in me the fullest measure of your confidence when I assure you that they were real. I have touched every centimeter of their silky, solid surface; stroked their palpable, factual perfection; kissed and adored every plane and pore and piggy.

And so you see, having known the Ideal incarnate, I was loath to accept less when it came to choosing a life's partner. Having fed on honeydew and drunk the milk of Paradise, how could I settle for a burger and fries! Yet that was the only option on the menus I was presented by my dear, distracted parents.

What deplorable necessities shoes are! There are those, or so I'm told, who find intense erotic contentment in the agitated contemplation and tactile fondling of them. Well, far be it from me to knock another guy's neurosis. *De gustibus non est disputandum* I always say. But—how peculiar that anyone should prize the package and ignore the present, forget the content and go for the container. To what ingenious contrivances I was driven that I might view unshod the feet of the countless candidates presented for my inspection and approval. Sweet Mama was forever organizing balls, tedious galas at which nearly all of the eligible nubile contenders were wont to wear gowns that swept the floor and utterly concealed the objects of my searching but calculatedly unobtrusive gaze; and even when a higher hem allowed for a fleeting perusal, I could espy only shoes—stylish or sensible, pricey or prudent, large or small, basic black or colorful, but always and ever depressing, dreadful shoes. For reasons which will be transparent to you, patient reader and trusted confidant, but which unfortunately remained perplexing to my parents, I was forever suggesting seaside excursions or dips in the pool. (There is a delightful natatorium in our palace, a veritable fairyland—all pale, flickering emerald light and rich, ebbing echoes.) Kind Papa concluded that I had a mania for swimming, and indeed, I was an exceptional merman. In breast stroke and butterfly I represented my country at the summer Olympics—not, admittedly, so successfully as to "medal," but neither did I perform to my discredit.

By hook or by crook I managed to strip down and size up the feet of all those eligible female guests whose shoes even approached Eve's dainty, diminutive dimensions, but after years of frustration and disappointment I began to abandon hope. Not that they were all repellant. By no means. I enjoyed the contemplation of many a shapely ankle and stirring arch. But judged by Eve's lofty criteria, all were letdowns. Some few, indeed, were hideous—feet so insipid and characterless they might almost have induced me to revise my low opinion of shoes. Lady Peat, e.g., a simpering colleen, had bunions on her bulbous toes. Hannelore, the lubricious, surly scion of the Margrave and Margravine Schlectlaune, had a passable foot—and appalling peditosis. (Likewise Chastity, an ardent pubescent nympho, the comically nominated daughter of the Baron and Baroness Sagbottom. And the Princesse Bava-Saliva, whose involvement

FAIRY TALES FOR ADULTS

with a Sicilian mob boss—nicknamed the "Homicidal Hunk" by the lurid popular press—was later to create the juiciest *scandale* of the social season.) And Margaret Jones, heiress to the Criterion Steel fortune, "painted" her toes. What a shocking blunder—nay more, what a downright sin to conceal the ineffable, opalescent sheen of the God-given toenail under a gaudy veneer of "polish"! What an unaesthetic, absolutely anerogenic effect such an "improvement" produces. Compounding her original offense of using so atrocious a cosmetic, chatty Maggie bored me into a stupor with a wearisome disquisition upon all the "neat shades" commercially available: scarlet serenade, rufous rust, vermillion mist. This but a sampling of the extensive range of options in red. There are other hues as well, it appears. There is even—delicious antinomy—a neutral hue christened "nude"! Maggie's personal preference, the tasteless color brazenly exemplified on her toes as she developed her seaside lecture and I fought off sleep, was Cherokee blood. *Horreur*! And then there was the Portuguese divorcée who .... but enough! Perceptive, sympathetic, forbearing reader—you require no further illustrations to, as they say in the U S of A, "get the picture." And besides, I should have remembered: *Exempla sunt odiosa*.

However, sympathetic as I assume you are, my friend, it is not impossible—indeed it is positively likely—that, having perused my confession to this point, you might have wondered if my quest for the Perfect Foot controlled and dominated my life to the exclusion of all other interests and endeavors. It did not. I admit that I pursued my passion with uncommon zeal, but I also discharged the many and varied obligations of a royal prince with an exemplary assiduity that earned for me the praise of my parents and the devotion of my people. Nor did I fail to follow my poetic calling. I translated the complete poetry of my beloved Coleridge into graceful Bonovian meters. I indited a tragic "novel" in heroic couplets: twelve cantos composed in my own superbly melodious tongue, Bonovak—a long labor of love the completion of which consumed the stolen moments and leisure hours of nearly five crowded, fruitful years. An English "translation" of my *magnum opus* appeared illicitly (if not, strictly speaking, illegally: American/Bonovian copyright law being what it

175

is) under the ludicrous title *Magnum Opus*. This vile traducement is the work of an inglorious (but, alas, not mute) instructor at a dubious Appalachian institution of "higher" education dubbed Excelsior College. His absurd name is Bertrand B. Weakovid. A pettifogging, plodding, dull-witted pedant, a man whose knowledge of Bonovak is even more insecure than his comprehension of poetic meter, he produced a tin-eared, heavy-handed mangling of my frail, evocative, all-too-vulnerable stanzas. A virtual rape, outraged reader! And not only did he "translate" my poem into barbarous English, he "annotated" it: i.e. he hunts for nonexistent symbols and finds them; he discovers unintended "subtexts" and renders them explicit; he puts social and historical "background" into the foreground; he perceives "influences" from other poets—some of them insignificant scribblers of whom I have never heard. Do not buy his book, loyal reader! Or, better, buy it—and burn it!

(I may add, parenthetically, that despite his self-satisfied delight in finding bogus hidden meanings, the bumbling Weakovid failed to discover the poem's real secret—one which, as no one else is ever likely to discover it either, I may as well reveal. Here goes: if one jots down the first letters of the twelve cantos, he will have before him an anagram which, correctly unscrambled, will spell two Bonovian words which throw shafts of light on the otherwise mysterious conclusion to my versified novel. So now you know. Enjoy!)

But I digress. I must return to the main theme of my narrative, the central thread of my tapestry: my twinned epiphanic visions. Or, as Allito and her fellow citizens would put it in prosaic Americanese, my "sex life."

It was the twenty-fifth summer of my life. A superb summer. May. Fragrant breezes. Those dear little pale blue blossoms, *spritō graméta* (pixie gowns)—flora unique to Bonovia, or so I'm told by those more expert in botany than I—were in full, luxuriant bloom. Evening. The crepitation of invisible crickets. Across the waters of a tranquil lagoon, the nictitating lights of a distant casino. The prince—in a pearl-colored dinner jacket and lilac slacks. I was bored. Another of poor Mama's balls. I had retreated to the terrace to avoid the clamorous attentions of two of the most unsightly and insipid

FAIRY TALES FOR ADULTS

sisters I have ever set eyes on. I had ignited a cigarette, and as I exhaled, I saw—through a shifting, diaphanous cloud of smoke—indistinctly at first, but with increasing clarity—Eve/Allito! Eve in Allito. Allito as Eve. No no! I saw Allito. She was palpably, supremely herself. A vision so veridical that I knew in one thrilling moment of astonished recognition that my long, arduous search had at last been rewarded with unutterable, uttermost success.

She wore glass slippers! Stunned and incredulous reader, can you believe it? Can you conceive it? A shoe which showed the foot. Which, indeed, enhanced it—which lent a lustrous enchantment to the supple, soft flesh it encased. And her feet! Such feet! Feet the equals of which I had seen only once before and which—oh how richly is persistence rewarded!—I was, incredibly, indubitably seeing again.

This imperious vision enchanted my dazzled eyes and stirred within me breathless wonder.

I swept to her side and invited her to dance. We danced.

Time stood still. The busy earth paused in its ceaseless rotation. Even insistent lust attained a kind of serene equipoise, a breathless, transitory balance between anticipation and achievement.

Oh, what happiness—what delight!

I led her from ballroom to terrace where we might, once again, be alone. She ensconced herself on a chaise longue, elevating her feet so that they were fully available to my enamored gaze—a entrancing gesture the effects of which she seemed to be not entirely unaware.

"Your palace is a place and a half, prince. Compared to this set-up, I live in a dump."

Palace. A place. How cunningly the clever darling played with words.

"I'm delighted that you approve. Would you like me to show you about? There are some lovely chambers upstairs—salons, bedrooms."

"Sounds great, hon, but to tell ya the truth, I don't have much time. We'd better just sick to dancing."

And she smiled a smile—so ingratiating, so captivating! I was so besotted, so distracted by delight that the full implications of her remark failed to "register." To "sink in." To "ring a bell." (Notice, impressed reader, if you haven't already, my comprehensive mastery of Yankee lingo.)

Between her parted lips, a pastel pink bubble, glossy in the pale moonlight, emerged, grew great, and popped.

And then, do you know what that impish temptress did? No? She kicked off her shoes!

"My dogs are barking! These crystal suckers are hard on the tootsies."

What a captivatingly brilliant web of breezy, inventive words that ingenious girl could spin!

After a pleasant interval of small but stimulating talk, she re-slippered her feet and we danced once more. Indeed, I danced with no other partner that evening. We waltzed and polkaed and gavotted. She was—it's trite but true—light as a feather. I was happy as a lark. I was in seventh heaven. I was on cloud nine. I was getting two glasses of punch when . . . .

Where was she!

Was I cursed? Were my visions fated to dematerialize and disappear?

The clock was knelling midnight as I swept—frantic, frenzied—down the palace stairs. I reached the bottom in time to catch the glimpse of a retreating carriage.

A cry of anguished grief rang reverberant through the still summer air. Mine!

There on the stone step—truly, definitively there—was silent but eloquent testimony that my adored and adorable Allito had not been a dream. A single glass slipper! I picked it up, clasped it to my bosom, and vowed then and there that the rest of my life would be devoted to a ceaseless, single-minded search for the nymph whose faultless foot had worn it.

So, I assembled a cohort of aides and factotums, and set out for America. *Terra Incognita*.

Far were the distances we traversed in search of my lost Allito; wide is the country we explored. What curious wonders we encountered (the world's biggest paper clip, an elephant-shaped

FAIRY TALES FOR ADULTS

house, tar pits, a "land" bearing the name of a deceased animator, a "corn" palace, square-dancing tractors, a doll museum, large "miniature" golf courses, monumental Presidential faces on a cliff); what exotic food we consumed (pasties, piccalilli, "supreme" pizzas, JoJos, Tex-Mex tacos, Bar-B-Qed ribs, "chicken-fried" steak with "country" gravy, a-la-moded berry pies [boysen-, black-, blue—and huckle-], frozen "custard"); what peculiar place names, what piquant pronunciations we were met with (Greenwood, S.C.; Deadwood, S.D.; Paradise, Cal.; Hell, Mich.; Nothing, Ariz.; Loveland, Colo.; Sweetlips, Tenn.; Intercourse, Penn.; Climax, Minn.; Marseilles, Ill. [Used car sales/ In old Marseilles]; Terra Haute, Ind. [One's well advised to wear a coat/ In wintry, windy Terra Haute]; Gallipoli, Oh. [Is your gal a police woman?])! (How delightfully this dramatic quartet of terminal symbols—striving for and at last achieving perpendicularity—punctuates my bemused amazement!)

Oh, I could go on. We *did* go on. On and on.

All those "motels" we inhabited: all those pop-up bathtub plugs which won't pop down; the man-sized boxes that rumble like Etna and erupt cubes into cute little thermal "buckets"; the compact "makers" that brew a beverage one could only in an access of charity call "coffee"; coin-operated "magic fingers" that simulate seismic disturbances; lamps the illumination of which requires the precise calibration of a correct wall-switch option and the positioning of another switch maddeningly hidden somewhere upon the lamp itself; beds so "made" that the top sheet extends only to one's navel; walls designed for the delectation of eavesdropping deviants seeking second-hand erotic kicks. And the "art"! The sad clowns, the poker-playing dogs, the doe-eyed waifs, the blossom-gathering maidens. There was a particular velvet matador with his pretty little cap and tight buttocks who pursued me from coast to coast, assuming various graceful stances. Picking selectively from his many transmogrifications: he raised his sword in Bangor; steadied it in Wichita; and struck home in Tacoma.

But I shall (and here I employ a charming idiom taught me by a quick-witted waitress in Cheyenne [shy Ann])—"cut to the chase."

179

At long last we came to a shabby genteel residence inhabited by two vain sisters. They looked somehow familiar. The place was a dump. Pumpkin vines grew in the front yard and an assembly of nervy, noisy mice had convened a conference under the porch.

Savvy reader, let me candidly confess what you have already guessed. This business about shoe size was a farce. You may be assured that were I to catch even a transitory glimpse of Allito's inimitable foot, recognition would be so sudden and sure that a silly rigmarole involving a shoe would be completely irrelevant and unnecessary. However, as I was not in a position to admit as much, I relied upon that rigmarole as an inane but useful ruse.

Well, though they tried womanfully, the repulsive sisters could not insert their clodhopping feet into the petite slipper. Then, emerging from the kitchen, hair bedraggled and rag bedecked, came Allito! My heart stopped. My sly, exquisite, matchless darling gave me a quick, covert wink, effortlessly slipped on the slipper, thumbed her nose at her haughty, hideous siblings (merely step-sisters, I was to discover), and off we went to the nearest emporium to buy a snazzy trousseau.

We were married, dear reader. We have lived happily ever after. Patient Mama has taken endless pains—and not always unsuccessfully—to teach Allito courtly manners and queenly demeanor. And do you know what? You'll never guess. My irrepressible, irreplaceable wife, it turns out, loves shoes! She has bought hundreds of pairs. Not one of them glass. She loathes glass slippers. They were, it appears, loaned to her by a kindly but misguided godmother. I think no more highly of shoes than ever, but what does it matter that Allito dotes on them? I can afford to be indulgent. She is gloriously shoeless every night!

On the Skids

Jack Kerouac

I hadn't seen Henny Penny since we shacked up together with a gang of cons and derelicts in a flop on Chicago's south side. That was before she hooked up with Red Cockerel and took off to L.A. where, if Manny Eden told me right, she married Red, or maybe didn't, but in any case wound up turning tricks to support herself and him. Red left her, or so I heard, and for all I knew she was still out there, on the edge of the vast busy spinning American continent, still pursuing her unique and unpredictable Tao.

I'd just split with my live-in, Cindymae, but I'm not going to tell about that. It would be a long gruesome tale, and anyway it was over. It had all come to a loud door-slamming dish-smashing climax, and I had relegated it to my merry madman past. No regrets.

Henny showed up at my Brooklyn pad late one hot summer night. I was sweating away over my novel in which—though she didn't know it—Henny was one of the characters. And, trust me, she was always one of life's great characters, the only kind I like, eager souls who pursue their upshining and avid outlooking through all the looming and sordid thisandthats. She burned with a fierce sapphire acetylene flame, ever ready to cut right through the hard steel surface to the suffering pure living center, to travel down the long sad streets of all the cities, looking, wanting and questing, spending and not counting costs, moving, moving, until like a runaway wildfire she burned it all up and the people around her said "Whoa!"

"Henny!" I said. "You crazy gone chick!"

"Cocky, love! Bet you didn't expect to clap eyes on me again—didn't think I'd turn up like a bad penny, did ya? Hee, hee."

She was flat broke and needed a place to crash. I told her she'd always have a place in my heart and on my sofa

"Hot *damn*! Let's get busy and start *talkin'*."

She pulled a bottle of panther piss out of her duffle and we got crocked, reminiscing and deliberating like two karma obsessed pilgrims, summoning up out of the deep well of Memory the frolics and follies of our long-gone ever-present past. Seems that Red, who never married her, ditched her in San Antone where before his vanishing act he pushed drugs and panhandled while she slung hash in some greasy spoon. "He hit the rails, or thumbed his way outta town—who knows? One day he just up and went with the wind. I haven't a clue where the sonofabitch is now?" Since then she had worked in a house in Dallas, spent some time in Vegas where she parlayed a few bucks into a small fortune at the blackjack table but lost it all at the roulette wheel, taken up with a sweet-mannered dim-witted traveling salesman who was a phenomenal success at flogging Bibles to hicks and who wanted to marry her but couldn't because he was already stuck with a wife back in Biloxi who was vicious as a junkyard bitch and wouldn't give him a divorce, fell in with a Zen mystic and spent a few months in a California ashram contemplating her navel, took a Greyhound to New York and studied method acting with an over-the-hill actor whose theories about achieving an intimate identification of actor and character ultimately involved getting intimate with him, lived in Greenich Village with a Negro musician who blew a mean horn and her meager bankroll, and—oh she traveled many another sunny path and shady byway and had adventures too numerous to recount.

But all this was just prelude, foofaraw and fanfare leading up to the Main Point which was that while she was lying low in Colorado trying to shake the fuzz, who were on her tail because she had stolen a couple of cars, one in the Big Easy, which she totaled,

FAIRY TALES FOR ADULTS

and another in Saint Louie, which conked out in Cody, Wyoming, where she hitched a ride with a bull-doggin cowboy riding the rodeo circuit who drove her straight down to Denver's Larimer street, one of her haunts, where she moved in with a bird named Dee Dee Daddles, whom her friends called Ducky because that's the way she always thought that everything was, she had a vision. She became tremendously excited when she told me about it. She got up and paced to the window and back, to the window and back, she raised her eyes to the skies and ran quivering fingers through her beautiful silken hair, she chirped and chortled with girlishglee, she worked herself into an excellent joy-making frothfrenzy. She had gone to Central City with Dee Dee and some of her gang where, in this old mining town opera house they have there, they heard Tosca pour out her passion in pure shining glory tones before she jumps into the Tiber. Then they went to a bar, took up with a couple of stagehands and got invited to the cabin of the guy playing the part of Angelotti who only sings in the first act and gets to go home early. It was a swell place a couple of miles up some canyon. There were twenty or so people at this impromptu BYOB party, all getting smashed and making out. Well, old Henny, who was fagged out from two days of non-stop partying, suddenly felt an overwhelming desire for a long lovely monster sleep. She staggered outside and saw in the subtle silver moonlight a huge oak tree under which she collapsed and fell into the black deep wooly womb of the immense unfathomable Unconscious.

And when she woke up . . . . But that's the thing. She didn't wake up like anyone usually wakes up—squinty-eyed, mouth dry as a mummy's bones, head pounding like a trip-hammer. No, this was different. "Al-to-geth-er different, Cocky. Man, if I only had the words! The sun that morning dawned—well, actually, it was the middle of the afternoon: I must of slept ten, twelve hours—on a new day. On a new Henny, is more like it. Everything glowed, somehow, in a secret shiny pure light. It was like . . . . Oh, my brother, if I could only make you see it. I was floating in a crystal, and the things around me, the rocks and the grass, they were *holy*. Everything around me was God-made holymatter. And everything was clean—the dirt on the ground the bottles and cans and refuse and crud in the garbage can and even the bird poop on the cement driveway—it was all clean. And it always had been clean only my *eyes* had been smudged and cloudy like dirty glasses."

"Henny, honey, how much pot had you smoked?

"Oh, earlier I had been high as a kite on rotgut and hash, naturally, but this wasn't that. All that had worn off. This was a conve*r*sion, man! And it wasn't any flash-in-the-pan epiphany either. I stayed high on holymatter for *hours*. Fact is, I'm high now—as I speak. Not *as* high—because I think that if you always felt as peaceful and blissful as I did then, you'd be—I don't know—dead and gone to heaven, I guess. But, trust me, once your eyes get cleaned by God's pure lovelight that shines like a black flame even in the darkest dark they *stay* cleaned. And you know what—and you can believe this or not—you know how we always think that the sky's up there and we're down here? Well, I'm telling ya, that's not the way it is at all. The sky goes up up infinitely far, yes, *but*—it also goes down too. Right down to the middle of the earth. And it goes through everything and everybody. It's *in* us. It's in you and me and everyone. We're all made of sky. I walk around on sidewalks and look at all the sad earnest toiling people rushing by and I know that they're sky people. But they don't know it. And that's a cryin' miserable shame because if the earth comes to an end anytime soon—and one of the things I now know for sure is that *that's* not impossible—they would all be frightened and downcast. And there's no *need*. Because we're all—ah, yes!—sky people, and the sky doesn't come, *can't* come, to an end."

Now I'm going to say something about Henny's father, and the reason I'm going into this subject is that it ties in with everything Henny and I did together after we hooked up and set out on our journeys. The father was a down-and-out wino named King Penny. That was his name not because his caved-in sadsack features were in any way regal but because the outlandish moniker his folks pinned on him was *Kingsblood*, and he went with a shortened version of that because he thought, I guess, that that would be a little less ridiculous and inappropriate. I saw him once, years ago. He was sitting on a park

FAIRY TALES FOR ADULTS

bench in the soft magenta twilight of a Denver summer evening. Henny introduced us, but I doubt if he ever really saw me. Drunk as he was, he made a little joke. It wasn't a funny joke, but still—getting even a feeble witticism out of that sad old souse was as surprising and wonderful as getting a piece of real information from discarded blown-away begrimed scrap of newspaper. Henny asked him if he was high on hash—hash being, next to vino, his favorite avenue to Nirvana—and he said he was a high as the city. Which made no sense to me until I remembered that Denver is called the mile-high city. I always remember that experience—that weary wasted enduring journeyman on Life's worn and pitted highway, sitting on the park bench where he planned to spend the night, cracking a fantastic stupid joke.

Henny's mother lost her life in childbirth, so whenever Henny was living with her father, her mothering, if any, was provided by whatever goodtime Charlene or barroom chippy King happened to pick up along the way. She was drug up in crummy hotels and sleazy dives in burgs all over the West—Denver mostly. A mason by trade, King found work when he looked for it, but he never looked for work as hard as he looked for the nearest waterhole. He was had up for vagrancy so often that knew the insides of half the stirs from Butte to Tucumcari. Sometimes, for a few months at a time, Henny lived in Cheyenne with her mother's sister, an old maid schoolmarm, a lady of steel will and spectacles who was a fire-and-brimstone Evangelical, a stern disciplinarian, and a closet lush. What little Henny ever saw of a settled way of life she saw in her aunt's house. The aunt wouldn't have anything to do with her brother-in-law, wouldn't speak to him or even mention his name, and till the day she died, which was sometime during Henny's tenth year on this lonely spaced-out vertiginous planet, her aunt tried to poison Henny's mind against her Paw—that's how Henny invariably referred to her father. But the aunt never succeeded. And that was one grand and beautiful thing about Henny. Old King Penny treated her like dirt, but she was always completely convinced that he loved her—even though he often forgot about her, mistreated her, and finally even, when she was a young teenager, abandoned her. She hadn't seen her

185

DAVID R. EWBANK

Paw in years and had no idea where he was. She couldn't even be sure that the old guy was alive. It seemed to me that his liver would be so pickled by all the alcohol he'd swilled that he would likely have kicked the bucket long since, but Henny wouldn't believe it. She just knew that he was still living. Maybe he'd be unconscious in a gutter when she finally found him, but she had firm faith that somewhere, sometime she would find him alive and breathing.

And that's what was behind the proposal she then presented to me which was that we take off and go looking for King. She had gotten it into her dream-dizzy head that if she could only find him and inform him of his sky nature she could confer such a life-altering bliss-fraught blessing on the old guy as the world hadn't seen nor heard tell of since Paul was struck with a staggering bolt of blinding vision on the road to Damascus. And she wasn't to be deterred by any nit-picking remarks like "Your Paw's probably dead" or "Even if he isn't, you have the same chance of locating him in a country as big as America as a sailor has of finding a particular fish in the ocean." That street-saintly crazy-wayed holywoman just brushed all that aside like a speck of dust. She *knew* she was fated to find her Paw.

"But, Henny, I'm bottomly broke, and so are you."

"Everything's fine! Dee Dee's gonna grubsteak us. Dee Dee's in Jersey, as I speak, visiting her brother, but she'll be joining me soon. She's got some dough. She earned a few bucks servin' Joe and franks to road-weary bruisers at a big truckstop outside of Omaha—ballin' a few johns on the side. And she's got wheels too. She bought a battered old jalopy when the two of us wiled away a few months down in Sarasota. But that's another story. Dee Dee and I got involved with Ping and Pong, the Siamese twin circus act, and followed them to their winter home. But it didn't last. It mighta worked out for Dee Dee and Pong, but when I found out from Pong that Ping was cheatin' on me with the bareback rider, Ping called Pong a lousy snitch and beat him up so bad that he had to go to the hospital. Ping forgot that he'd never have to worry about observing limited visiting hours. Hee hee."

Well there's no resisting the call of the road, especially when that call comes from a mad ecstasycrazed Maenad like Henny. When a

186

FAIRY TALES FOR ADULTS

couple of days later, just about suppertime, Dee Dee pulled up in a battered but unbowed Dodge sedan, I piled inside with a cardboard suitcase in my hand, my heart as light as my wallet, keen for whatever the future might bring. It's like Henny says, what do you want out of life if not the whoosh and swish of pure pristine air sweeping up and over the huge swelling curve of our hallowed way-wending American continent, slapping your face and messing your hair as you bend toward the promise of tomorrow, eagering for the road ahead, looking always toward the prime peerless consummation around the bend as you drive, dive, and keep on drivin—whah! whoo!—heading for that ineluctable and insuperable WHATEVER!

Dee Dee was an A-one hardliving freewheeling American saint. That realgone thrillhungry cookie just barreled on down life's long long trails, swacked on happy juice and hold on Hannah. She just didn't give a damn. She had a heart as soft as eiderdown, and if Henny hadn't put her foot down, would have stopped to pick up every roadside waif and wastrel aiming to get across the country on his or her thumb. She hadn't had a license more than a couple of months, but she took to driving like a duck takes to water. She plopped down in the driver's seat, let out a spiritslifting earsplitting whoop, floored that chromium chariot, and—wham—we *moved*. Unfortunately, as it turned out, Dee Dee wasn't nearly as well funded as she had led Henny to believe, but she was always just as willing as any of the rest of us to pitch in and steal or earn some moolah so that she could contribute to the communal kitty.

First gas station we came to I got to talking to a down and out exotic dancer, Miss Poosy, who was unemployed because the dive where she was struttin' and strippin' got raided and boarded up. Some of her colleagues were running a lucrative little side business banging the superheated voyeurs. Miss Poosy was a knockout—long luscious legs that wouldn't quit and knockers big as balloons. But was that poor sweetheart ever cheated in the greymatter department! Jeezus what a goose! That nice naïve innocent dim broad didn't know her ass from her elbow. But that was all right; any chick with an ass as sweet as hers isn't often called upon to draw subtle distinctions.

Miss Poosy was on her way to Cleveland where she knew a guy who had a brother who owned a club and could probably give her some work, if not as a stripper, then as a B-girl. So, she knew at least where she was going, but she lacked the way and wherewithal, so I suggested that she ride with us to Cleveland, a suggestion which she gladly accepted. This arrangement, made without her involvement or approval, ruffled Henny's feathers. She clucked and scowled and stalled for a few minutes, but in the end she came around and we all four sped off into the mystic American night.

Well, we got over the Jersey border to Parsippany before the Dodge shuddered and groaned and gasped and gave up the ghost. A gas station mechanic told us to forget about repairing it—said we'd be lucky to find a junk dealer who'd be willing to take such a useless old rustbucket. So there we were, four hopeful wayfarers on our way to Oz, stalled after our first baby step up the yellow brick road. Alas and alack!

But Miss Poosy saved the day. She had a "friend," T. L., who lived, she thought, in Newark. Wasn't that in Jersey? Well, then, she could give him a call and see if he couldn't drive over to Parsippany, pick us all up, and take us on to Cleveland.

Henny and Dee Dee thought that this was about as likely as a flying saucer swooping down to give us a lift, but I said what the hell, give it a try. So Miss Poosy shimmied and swayed on her spike heels over to a pay phone and, using a fistful of change we gave her, placed a call to one Tom Lurky, and I'm damned if that crazy cat didn't agree, not only to get us to Cleveland, but to join us on our cross country search for King. Likewise Miss Poosy, because when we pulled into Cleveland neither the guy with the brother nor the club-owning brother himself was anywhere to be found. And that turned out to be a good thing because three or four time when we ran out of gas and money on our mad meandering coast-to-coast trek, Miss Poosy was the one who earned us some quick cash by employing her various professional talents.

When T. L. pulled up in front of the tacky fleatrap where we had crashed for the night, he extricated his long bulky frame out from under the steering wheel of a snazzy new Buick convertible

FAIRY TALES FOR ADULTS

and introduced himself by giving us all a big bear hug. He right off declared that he was altogether free of entanglements—vocational, conjugal or sentimental—and ready to roll. Man oh man, I said to myself, have we ever fallen into a pot of jam! Tom—"Turkey," he called himself, because he said that, being constitutionally incapable of shooting the bull, that was the only kind of talk he could talk—was a good ole pot-bellied boy from Georgia. Well, maybe not such a boy. He was probably pushing forty, and he had a résumé as checkered as a hepcat's zoot suit. Bookie, used car salesman, barkeep, carney barker, pusher, warehouse guard, infantry sergeant, gandy dancer, fruit picker, pimp—you name any job on either the safe or the shady side of the law and old T. L. had probably spend at least a week or two of his manic peripatetic life at it. Looking at his fancy car and his corny but brand new cowboy duds (boots, fringed leather jacket, Stetson—the works), I though he was flush, but in that surmise I soon discovered I was mistaken. He must have blown all of his wad on wheels and threads because about three hundred miles down the pike he was as broke as the rest of us. He was a great talker, and I loved to hear the rambling narratives of his numerous escapades, even though, or maybe because, contrary to what he announced, half of what he said was the purest bullshit.

The five of us climbed into that highpowered streamlined heavensent gasbuggy and headed out on the longest craziest jazzride that ever tore up and barreled down the highways and lowways of this teeming dream-haunted American nation. In every city and town and hamlet we met sinners and Samaritans, conmen and holymen, thieves and saints and prophets. And everywhere we met dopeheads and drunkards and losers and liars of all sorts who said that they knew or knew of or had once heard of or had once seen King Penny. Since the object of our quest, assuming that he even existed, was known to be a man who was by preference habitually on the move, we were in the unlucky position of trying to hit a moving target while moving ourselves. But hell—it's the going not the getting there that counts! If King was the goal that got us going, then I was willing to believe in the guy, even if I had my doubts about ever clapping eyes on him.

A brokendown whiskeyleg in Fort Wayne told us he'd seen King in a hobo camp in Knoxville, so we went down there. In Dallas, a nightclub hipster said he knew a guy who had met a guy name of King when he was doing time for auto theft in Pontiac, so we rushed up to the Illinois state pen. A prostitute in Des Moines was sure she'd run across a man named King when she was up in Detroit, working, and he was employed as a bricklayer on a federal housing project, so guess where we went next. We followed bogus leads and false tips to Fargo, North Platte, Casper, Denver, Flagstaff, Provo, Boise, Winnemucca, and Reno until finally we hit Frisco and ran out of land. We wheeled and staggered and veered across the country like a hopheaded bumblebee. We searched the tumbledown garrets and reeking gutters of bustling cities and jerkwater burgs from sea to shining sea, but in not one did we ever find King. We did find adventure aplenty. We saw mountains and plains and deserts and fertile valleys. We talked to workers and bums and men of the cloth and ladies of the night. We saw the insides of mansions and jails. We shot the bull with sots and Senators. (Well just one Senator.) I took temporary jobs as dishwasher, store clerk, barkeep, bouncer, floor sweeper, field hand, hackie and hard hat—to mention only my legitimate billets. Fantastic, man! Every day was a pure beautiful sweet sacred day.

Well, when we got to Frisco we stopped for a few days to catch our breath, and in the mornings I started writing this epic of our cross-country trek. I had, at least temporarily, run out of the vim and vinegar it takes to start out on another quest. And anyway, I figured that Henny had probably finally given up trying to find her Paw. Dee Dee shocked and astonished us one day when she suggested that maybe it was time that we stayed put someplace and got steady jobs, but I quickly put the lid on that kind of talk. "Forget it," I said, "I'm beat."

But Henny has by no means given up on her search for King, and now, amazingly, our fortunes have taken an abrupt and unexpected turn. Last night in an all-night bistro where we hang out because a cool jazz combo blows long lovely ecstatic notes and you can buy margaritas and mary jane cheap, Henny met a lounge lizard,

FAIRY TALES FOR ADULTS

slicked down hair and sequins on the lapels of his dinner jacket, who claims that he not only knows King Penny, but knows where he's currently holed up—in an abandoned mine shaft down near Sutter's Mill. The guy goes by the phony alias Foxy Woxy. I wouldn't trust the glad-handing blowhard except for the fact that tomorrow he's offered to take us down there. None of the other lying lowlife tipsters have done that. I guess Foxy must be on the up and up.

So, live and learn. There's always another blessed day—another vision to amaze, another promise to be fulfilled. To the onrushing, ever-eager, never-consummated chronicle of my crazy crowded days it's still too early to write—the end.

192

The Paid Piper

Cormac McCarthy

They came in the beginning covert and stealthy and in such numbers as drew notice but stirred neither panic nor undue alarm among the citizens of the riverside town. The days of the early autumn were unwonted, intempestive. A westerly wind, frigid, bleak and pitiless, swept down from the blue vermiform sierras which defined the far horizon, and the common talk of the townsfolk when they met over mercantile counter or forgathered in church or saloon was more of severe weather impending than of imminent threat. Then the innkeeper's newborn son was found dead in his crib, his body unrecognizable and largely unrecoverable, the sheet upon which he had lain beslobbered with viscous gore and strewn with gobbets of flesh, quiescent testament to a massacre that had proceeded unnoticed and unimpeded because the attackers had in probability begun their feast at the infant's throat, and the mayor's maidservant was bitten while extracting potatoes from a bin in the fetid, unlit cellar of her master's house and within days lay in racking delirium, ulcerous pustules having erupted on her torso and limbs, and within weeks was dead, the first of a hecatomb whose protracted agonies and predestinate annihilation followed hard upon, and the granaries were aswarm with myriad, frenzied rodents that in their insatiate greed devoured within hours the rich surpluses of many harvests past, stored by the provident burgers against a day of need,

DAVID R. EWBANK

leaving only paltry remnants so fouled by and intermixed with turds as to be uncomestible, and then came days of famine, days of depravity: demand for the services of undertaker and gravedigger which had reached a pitch of frequency hitherto unprecedented began to slacken and at last to dwindle to nothing as ravenous survivors took to boiling and eating the bodies of their deceased kinfolk, nor did all of the starving abide the advent of natural mortality but hastened its coming by killing the newly afflicted, thus insuring a source of flesh more plentiful and potentially less tainted that that afforded by those whose illness had run its entire emaciating course, and indeed the practice of slaughtering the ill became so widespread that many stricken victims, at the first intimations of morbidity, took to arming themselves, regarding with suspicion the ministrations of even their closest family members, and the customary course of nature was still further disordered when the replenishment of the dwindling population through new births was abrogated by the practice of infant cannibalism, some famished and desperate wretches having discovered that from a meal of fresh baby meat, provided by infants either their own or not, could be derived nourishment superior to that attainable from two or three adult corpses, and so it was that murder, malicious and malevolent, came as a supplemental visitation to the shrinking population, inflicting miseries if not greater, then more starkly gratuitous and terrorful than the impartial sufferings, nescient and extrinsic, inflicted by the plague. Everywhere there were rats. Their numbers appeared to increase in inverse ratio to the declining food supply, a circumstance that confounded the vexed comprehension of the survivors. Though the townsfolk ceaselessly strove to annihilate the invaders by trapping, clubbing, and poisoning them, the appalling fecundity of the enemy, their blind persistence and the sheer magnitude of their predations rendered all resistance null and unavailing. It was as though a perdurable archetype, rat, assumed a rank and potency utterly superordinate to and independent of the fatal vicissitudes of its mortal instancing and was forever, by virtue of that inviolable status, unaffected by the frail exertions of human contriving.

Fairy Tales for Adults

In the harsh cold of a bitter November evening, a bloodred sunset lowering in the west, three men made their solitary ways from diverse points of origin through windswept streets toward their predetermined destination, the now vacant and derelict city hall—a large civic edifice untenanted except for swarming packs of rats which had taken up habitation in every room. Made brave by superior numbers, they no longer troubled themselves to avoid the presence of increasingly rare human intruders. Snakeskin, a tall, lean rancher with a livid scar on his cheek and three fingers missing on his right hand; Louie, a taciturn horse dealer, a relative newcomer who one day rode into town with a saddlebag stuffed with gold coins, inspiring widespread interest and comment, but whom, so violent was he of temper, so sullen of mood, no one cared to interrogate anent the enigma of his past history and present prosperity; Grunt, a retired army colonel who bore on his flaccid, obese, moonpale body scars accrued over several years in the many Indian Wars he had fought: these were the sole survivors of the town council which in days more auspicious had numbered fourteen, and they gathered to ponder once more the town's perilous plight, to consider what recourse, if one existed—what remedy, could one be devised, yet remained.

They came together without greeting and stood for some minutes, silent and morose, their breath turned to silvery vapor in the still, gelid air.

At last Louie leaned and spat.

"Ain't no use in this. Ain't nuthin' we kin do that ain't already been tried. We're damn nearit clean outta p'isin—not that what we tried already ever done much good."

"Might could try larger traps. Cages, like. Bait 'em and draw in a hunnert er so—then slam down the door on 'em," Snakeskin said.

"Bait 'em with what?" Grunt asked. "Ain't got enuf grub fer folks ta eat—let alone fer feedin' the rats—the greedy bastards. We ain't got no food ta spare."

"Mebbe we might bait with corpse meat. They'll eat that quick enuf."

DAVID R. EWBANK

No response was forthcoming to Louie's suggestion; none, indeed, seemed to be expected. Each man evaded the other's eye.

"We'd about as well piss in a rain barrel as try killin' the som'bitches."

As Grunt spoke, Snakeskin noticed upon the floor to his right a furtive shape advancing in his direction, cautious but deliberate, a rat, impelled by what bestial intent the vigilant man could well fathom, its evil eyes burning with cold, implacable malice. Awaiting the propitious moment, Snakeskin abruptly flattened with his heavy boot the head of the intruding rodent, instantly terminating the transcient, innominable life of the mortal creature, now as bereft of willful purpose as of sensate being. Regarding the pudding of blood and brains that lay by his foot, Snakeskin felt satisfaction only the most fleeting, the impotence of his accomplishment made manifest, even as the three men impassively examined its result, by a sly, scurrying sound, a constant sonance in the echoic, abandoned room, produced by the hundreds of rats yet alive and stirring.

"I can help you."

In the thickening darkness the speaker was scarcely discernable, but when he moved nearer, his viewers' astonishment at the presence of an onlooker was exceeded by the shock occasioned by his appearance. A small person, not more than five feet perhaps, he was clad in grey pants and shirt and a buff jerkin of antique cut, and withal so extravagant an assemblage of parti-colored patches that he seemed a fatuous, misled jester who took a conclave of desperate men to be a carnival.

At last it was Grunt who stifled his surprise and asked: "How you aim ta help us, mister?"

"My method is not at issue. My price is. One hundred pieces of gold."

His voice was high-pitched, his words oddly articulated.

"Where you hale from, stranger?" Snakeskin demanded. "Your talk's furrin. What makes you think you're dealin' with folk dumb enough ta believe ya?"

"What you gonna do we ain't already tried?" Louie asked. "Who are ya, and who asked ya ta come pokin' your long nose inta business ain't none a yours?"

196

FAIRY TALES FOR ADULTS

"Why don't you just take your skinny ass right on outa here," Grunt added.

"As you please gentlemen. But consider: I demand no payment until I've produced the promised results. If you have at your disposal means more effective, a plan more fitting for your purpose, why then I will, of course, happily oblige you by removing myself."

He waited not more than a minute. Hearing no response, he turned and began to retreat, but just before he reached the door Louie spoke out.

"Wait!"

Addressing his two companions, Louie said: "What the hell! The guy's crazy, but what have we got ta lose? We ain't got no food left, more than half the people in town's dead, and them that ain't is dyin'. The one thing this town's got, locked up in the treasury, is gold. That's the one thing safe from the rats 'cause they can't eat it. And what we gonna do with it? This here crack-brained blatherskite's no doubt full a shit, but if he can get rid of the goddamn rats, why—he'd more than *earn* his pay."

Perceiving no flaw in this logic, Snakeskin and Grunt made no demur, and the three council members forthwith promised to the outlandish stranger the sum on one hundred gold coins were he able to make good on his promise to rid the town or rats.

"You got a handle a man kin use ta call ya by, mister?" Louie inquired.

"Piper."

The import of this terse retort did not become apparent till the men, following the stranger out into the twilight, watched as he extracted from a leather purse depending from his shoulder a slender wooden fife which he set to his lips and commenced to play. A keen, eldritch sound, not loud but astringent, came pouring forth, boring into the gathering darkness a shaft of pellucid melody which imposed upon all else in that derelict street a primed, quickening silence. A breathless hiatus, as though an implacable decree arrested and held in awed suspense the ceaseless impetus of onward-tending time. Then, a clamorous pandemonium as from doors, windows, attics, cellars and subterranean warrens a torrent of rapt, avid rats streamed into the street and pursued in their rampant haste—not, or so it seemed, the retreating figure of the piper, though he was moving steadily away from the three townsmen, never ceasing as he marched to sustain his piping—but the piping itself which assumed a reality independent of its physical source, piping which, ideal and increate, employed the piper as an opportune, temporary conduit so that its fatal influence might accommodate and effect the fitful phenomenal world. A river of vermin, hundreds and hundreds of the restive, gripped creatures scampered headlong at the heels of their piebald leader, the one composed and stolid member of the grotesque promenade, wholly unperturbed by the riotous chaos of his making. Reaching the end of the street he turned and led his train of brutish, bewitched attendants to the brink of a swollen river which rushed between steep, narrow banks. There he came to a stop, though the fey, eerie air he produced on his fife persisted, and there the rats in their teeming numbers leapt into the coursing water like keen, fervent proselytes mad for some supreme abnegative apotheosis. The turbulent water turned grey with numberless rats thrashing and straining in their anonymous death agonies, but within minutes it ran unencumbered again, swift and lethal, but with its wonted clarity.

A queer silence had settled over the town when the lone piper reappeared on the town's street. Those inhabitants who had survived the plague, astounded by the sudden miraculous exodus, now stood on their doorsteps or leaned from windows and gaped in witless wonder at the strange personage making his hasteless way toward the three councilmen. He had ceased his piping.

"My pay, if you please, gentlemen. One hundred gold coins."

He extended his hand, palm upward, toward his dazed and incredulous employers.

A long, suspenseful moment ensued.

"Well, I 'low as how ya done what ya promised." It was Snakeskin who spoke at last. "Hold on. We'll have ta fetch the gold from the safe inside."

With a jerk of his head he indicated that the town's treasury was within the walls of the city hall, and he turned to enter the building.

Fairy Tales for Adults

"Hold on yurself!" Louie demanded. "Don't be so quick ta hand out money that don't belong ta ya."

"Don't belong ta me nor you neither—now," Snakeskin retorted. "Belongs ta this piper fellow. It's like ya said yurself: if he can kin do what he said he'd do, he'd *earn* the money."

"Why, shit! What did the man *do*? Nuthin'! Just played a little tune on his—whatever the hell ya call it. That ain't man's work. We never said we'd pay out fer a magic show."

"Rats is gone, ain't they? What's it matter how?"

"Louie's right," Grunt interposed. "Pipin' ain't worth a hunnert. Give 'em five gold pieces, call it tip and tell 'im ta clear outta town."

This attempt at compromise was ineffective, pleasing neither Snakeskin, who insisted upon honoring his word, nor Louie, who considered the expenditure of five gold pieces to be as exorbitant as it was unnecessary.

"Louie," Snakeskin said, "I ain't about ta set still for this. I'm gonna go in there and get the dough. If you aim ta stop me, you're gonna have ta shoot me."

With a swift, deft sweep on his hand, Louis drew his six shooter from its holster and placed a bullet squarely between Snakeskin's eyes. Snakeskin stood stark and still for a second or so, his brains dribbling out a gaping hole at the rear of his head like bloody drool dripping from the maw of a rapacious carnivore. In the seconds before Snakeskin fell backward, stiff as a felled tree, Louis, mistakenly assuming that one bullet had been insufficiently fatal, fired off three more. Two reduced Snakeskin's face to a gory pulp, the first ripping through his right eye, the second hitting his mouth, causing a explosive spray of teeth to scatter over the dumb and unresisting earth. A third bullet went over Shakeskin's shoulder as it plummeted downward and hit in the chest a bystanding widow whose attempt at a scream was aborted by a stifled gasping for air, a desperate inhalation which produced only an odd crooning wail. She slumped against the doorpost by which she was standing, slid to the ground and died.

Pale red rays of the sinking sun illuminated the impassive face of the piper as he turned to address those townsfolk within range of

199

his voice. His tone was neither threatening nor angry, yet his words reverberated, chilling and portentous, in the vacant air.

"Citizens, I have been promised one hundred gold coins for ridding your town of rats. I have performed that service and now expect to be given my reward. If you refuse to pay me the money I have honestly earned, I give you fair warning: a grievous misfortune will befall you. I *will* be paid—if not in coin, then in condign revenge."

For several long minutes the piper stood stock still awaiting a response. He gave no sign of pique or impatience. His face, indistinctly ruddy in the dying light, was fixed, blank. Though his eyes were open, they seemed to be sightless—the stone eyes of an ancient sphinx.

When at last he moved, having elicited no response, he wordlessly removed the fife from his purse and began to play upon it. A keening, droning tune, strange and disturbing, cut like a sharp knife through the thickening darkness. And when the weird, elfin musician began to move slowly and deliberately down the street, all the children of the town, drawn by invisible bonds, stepped forth and followed him. The parents were as deeply, though differently, affected: they stood wonderstruck and transfixed, robbed not of the will, but of the power to intervene in the awful spectacle transpiring like an implacable fatality before their astonished eyes.

Soon the children were out of sight, lost in the deep, enveloping night. When they were all gone, there could still be heard for a few brief moments, ringing like a distant echo, the thin, frail strains of the piper's fading song.

When dawn broke bleak and cheerless over the desolated village, a solitary figure appeared, walking with slow, halting steps up the empty street. It was the blacksmith's crippled son. As soon as he was spotted a throng of eager parents congregated about him, and to them he related the appalling and wonderful story of his companions' being led by the piper into a vast black hole in the side of

FAIRY TALES FOR ADULTS

a mountain. Once they had filed inside, the cavern had miraculously closed, trapping its captives inside. The narrator, impeded by his slow, limping gait, arrived upon the scene just in time to view that awesome closure.

The weeping mother knelt and embraced her child.

"Son, what made ya hanker so ta follow that piper man?"

"It was his music, ma."

"It was peculiar music sure enough. Did it tempt ya cause it put ya in mind of lollipops and ice cream and such?"

"Oh, no. It put me in mind of slaughterin' and war and the sheddin' of blood."

"Why, land sake, son. What's temptin' about them things?

"Oh, ma. If you could only have heard what I did. That piper fellow put inta his tune such lovely-soundin' didoes and fancy trills—he made it sound soooo purdy!"

Printed in Great Britain
by Amazon.co.uk, Ltd.,
Marston Gate.